1975

Anthology of Mexican Poetry

*Unesco collection
of representative works:
Latin American Series.
Published with
the cooperation of
the Organization of
American States*

Anthology
of
Mexican Poetry

compiled by OCTAVIO PAZ

translated by Samuel Beckett

preface by C. M. Bowra

INDIANA UNIVERSITY PRESS

BLOOMINGTON & LONDON

THIS anthology is published by agreement between Unesco and the government of Mexico as part of a program of translations of representative works undertaken by Unesco. The anthology was compiled by Octavio Paz, who has also contributed, at Unesco's request, a study of Mexican poetry. In an entirely different spirit, Unesco asked Professor C. M. Bowra to introduce this book to the English-speaking public, and M. Paul Claudel to perform a similar service for French readers. Their essays should not be considered as prefaces or introductions in the usual sense. They are intended rather to emphasize the essential solidarity of creative artists in different nations, languages, centuries, and latitudes, and to point out the fundamental identity of emotions to which the genius of the poet can give a form at once lasting and beautiful.

TRANSLATOR'S NOTE: I SHOULD LIKE TO THANK MR. GERALD BRENAN FOR KINDLY READING THE ENTIRE MANUSCRIPT AND FOR MAKING A NUMBER OF USEFUL SUGGESTIONS.   S.B.

EIGHTH PRINTING 1971

0-253-29929-2   cl 253-10390-8

Contents

Poetry and Tradition

It can hardly be claimed that the advance in material civilization has done much for poetry. The growth of large towns has curtailed that intimate connection of man with nature which has in the past provided countless themes for song; the pressure of crowded populations fosters conventions of behavior which are inimical to the free play of imaginative 'impulse; the spread of standardized education does not always encourage the originality and independence which are necessary to creative work; the specialization of intellectual life diminishes not merely the desire to write poetry but the ability to enjoy it. A mass of evidence shows that poetry is far less popular in western Europe and the United Sates than in countries like Persia or China or India, whose material civilization is far less advanced but which have kept a traditional taste for the beauty of words. In societies where conditions are still more primitive and existence is indeed hard, poetry may be the main pastime and consolation of peoples like the Asiatic Tartars or the Armenians or the Ainu, among all of whom it is a truly national art practiced with a high degree of accomplishment and enjoyed by whole populations. Compared with such societies our own mechanized, urban world is indeed feeble and uncertain in its approach to an art which has in the past enjoyed great glory but seems now in danger of becoming an esoteric pursuit of cliques and coteries.

The situation may even be worse than this. Some of our popular prophets foresee a time when poetry will almost have disappeared because there will be no demand for it, or at the best will have become a specialists' pastime like chess or an antiquated superstition like astrology. It is assumed that the analytical, scientific spirit which informs so much modern thought will have replaced the old imaginative, poetical spirit which seeks to produce a synthesis of experience and to present any given situation as a concrete whole. To these gloomy presentiments the recent history of poetry gives some support. By becoming more intimate and more difficult, poetry has lost some of its old public and has not yet trained a new public to take its place. In its desire to convey the subtler, more elusive movements of the consciousness it tends to avoid the broad issues which have often given it strength in the past and to concentrate on aspects of experience which are sometimes so special that they can be fully understood by few but the poets themselves. In abandoning much of its old territory and relinquishing it to science or history or theology, poetry makes itself less approachable even to those who wish to enjoy it.

This contraction of poetry is a matter of grave concern. At the lowest level, we may deplore that an art which for countless centuries has given pleasure to multitudes should lose much of its power and find no adequate successor; for few will claim that the novel or the drama or the cinema can do what poetry does or in any sense take its place. If poetry is really shrinking, we may well lament that a great joy is being taken from us and that the art of living will be correspondingly impoverished. But of course the loss would be far worse than this. Poetry is much more than a source of pleasure, more even than a source of joy in the highest and purest sense; it is an essential element in civilization and does much to preserve and enliven it. Since any civilization worthy of the name is much more than a technical application of scientific discoveries and is of no importance unless it brings enrichment to our inner lives, it is dangerous to dispense with poetry or even to reduce its influence. A world without poetry is perfectly conceivable, but it would not be worth living in. Not only would it be bleak and barren; it would lack valuable qualities which we do not always associate with poetry but which it discovers and keeps alive and makes essential elements in the richness and variety of life.

Poetry lives by tradition. It derives from the past not merely its consciousness of its own nature and function but much of its technique and outlook. In doing this it not only keeps alive great discoveries made in the world of spirit but makes new discoveries of a similar character for its own age. The tradition of poetry is alive and adaptable in the same way as a tradition of manners. It faces new problems with well-tried instruments and secures new results from them. Though it can never repeat exactly what has been done before, since in poetry, as in all the arts, mere repetition is bound to be dead and useless, it can do in a new way the same kind of thing that has often been done, and its success lies in the new approach and the new vision which it brings to the individual event in the given, recognized field. Like all true traditions, that of poetry selects something significant from the particular scene, preserves this for posterity, and continues to make a similar selection whenever it has a chance of doing so. But traditions are delicate organisms and if they are treated too roughly they cease to do their right work. So if poetry breaks too violently with the past and conducts experiments in too reckless a spirit, it may well hurt itself. Indeed it is difficult not to think that something of this kind has happened in our own time, which has surely been rich in talent but has not quite produced the poetry demanded or deserved by our circumstances. However this may be, it remains true that poetry lives by tradition, and that such a tradition is important not merely for poetry but for anything that may rightly be called civilization.

One of the chief claims of poetry as a civilizing influence is that it presents in a lasting and persuasive form the discoveries which man has made about himself and his circumstances, about the possibilities and the significance of events seen with clairvoyant vision and passionate intensity. The poets whose work survives the corroding influence of time express something so important that it becomes part of ourselves, even though we may be divided from them by many centuries. In such a process the expenditure is of course enormous. For every poem that endures, thousands and thousands perish, and even in the work of great poets there may be much that is remembered only because of the good company it keeps. This process not only reflects the capacity or otherwise of poets to say something worth saying as it should be said, but determines the final worth of their achievement, as time and succeeding generations test and judge it. The business of selection goes on until only what is beyond cavil survives, but this is of inestimable worth and forms an essential part of living history.

How poetry chooses and preserves experience may be seen from a glance at some great works in which the poet gives life to what has most touched or stirred him in fact or legend or belief and arms it with an appeal which moves far beyond his contemporary setting to an almost timeless world. The *Iliad,* for instance, is the last word on the heroic world of ancient Greece. In it the concept of heroism, the idea that a man should devote his life to the display of prowess and the acquisition of glory, provides the central theme and the main setting. Achilles is a hero almost without peer. Sigurth may equal him in prowess but is inferior to him in humanity; Roland may be equally tragic but is certainly not so foursquare. In Achilles the heroic way of life is presented in all its implications, its taste for action and its sense of personalities, its magnificent manners and its inevitable doom. Once Homer had composed the *Iliad,* no other poems could hope to challenge him on such a theme. It is the climax of Greek heroic society and must have been composed when that society was already beginning to be transformed into something else. But just for that reason it presents what matters most in such a world, and the wonderful paradox is that, though we have passed far from any heroic age, Homer's world is still perfectly real to us, not merely in the sense of being vivid and present but in the sense of making us feel toward its characters what we might feel toward our own friends and acquaintances. Only our feelings toward them are less confused and less cloudy than in any ordinary existence. The art of poetry has made its selection not merely from story but from the complex mass of human nature and found in this what it thinks to be most exciting and moving. Homer gives us something invaluable just because he operates with a world which we do not know, and yet, when he presents it, we see it to be somehow intimate and familiar.

What Homer does for heroic Greece, Dante does in his own remarkable way for the Middle Ages. Into the *Divine Comedy* he put not only the science, philosophy, theology, and literary criticism of his time, but his own highly individual judgments on men and things. He surveys all history as he knows it from the Bible, the Roman historians, and his own chroniclers, presents its achievements through his own highly discriminating, highly critical judgment, and makes it live through the power of his poetical vision, with the result that it is difficult for us, with our far greater sources of knowledge, to see some characters except as Dante saw them. He has given the final portraits of such men as Farinata or Pietro delle Vigne, and, more than this, he presents through his art a coherent conception of life which people find relevant even today. Even if we do not accept his main assumptions, we must still feel that his is a point of view of absolute value, that if we absorb it we shall understand life better than we do and be aware of much which we habitually neglect. Of course the *Divine Comedy* is the work of an almost unique genius, but it derives part of its strength from the world in which Dante lived and which he examined with so sharp an understanding that what mattered most in it is still alive for us today.

If poetry preserves the continuity of civilization by passing to coming generations what matters most in its discoveries, so also it shapes the future by seeing where tendencies still obscure and generally unmarked may lead and what their fulfillment means. It is not too much to claim that, if in Achilles Homer created the exemplar of heroic valor, he created in Hector the champion of the city-state which had hardly emerged in his time and was to dominate the Greek scene for centuries. If Dante was much concerned with the characteristics of individual Italian towns, he had also a vision of a united Italy which was to dominate men's imaginations for centuries until at last it was realized in fact. Some poets do more than this. Their vision pierces into the distance and sees forms which even they themselves may not fully understand or appreciate, but which through their presentation of them in due course come into being. Though Virgil tells of Rome as it was in the beginning, he looks forward to a future of order and peace, which was indeed to exist over the Roman world for some two centuries, and beyond this he descries less firmly but not less sincerely certain doubts and misgivings about man's place in the universe which were later to trouble Marcus Aurelius and to do much for the triumph of the Christian Church. In this sense poetry is indeed a kind of prophecy, but what it foretells are not events but movements of the spirit, the emergence of hitherto unrecognized powers of the will and intelligence, stirrings in the heart which will change the texture of human life and open vast new vistas to the imagination and affections.

This power to preserve the past and to foresee the future belongs in a special degree to Shakespeare and accounts for the simple but not disreputable belief that in him all knowledge that is worth having is to be found. From one angle we see that he comes at the end of a great period, which he presents in all its richness and inner life. He is indeed the poet of the English Renaissance, which was itself in many ways the culmination of the English Middle Ages. Just as in his historical plays he presents English history from Richard II to Henry VI, so in his own thought he covers a wide range of speculation which touches at one end the ageless, ancient legends of his people and at the other the daring speculations of his own time. The crowded present which he saw and marked with such vivid discrimination provides much of the matter in Shakespeare's plays, but at the same time he follows many unsuspected clues in himself or his acquaintances until he develops themes which

were new to his world and have not yet exhausted their fresh-
ness, though they have indeed affected the course of history
and created new types of men. Hamlet, for instance, may well
contain much that Shakespeare knew in himself, but has en-
abled many men of later generations to see themselves more
clearly and to diagnose their own maladies. Without him much
French or Russian literature of the nineteenth century could
hardly have been written, and indeed the very type of Hamlet
is established in our technique of understanding our fellows.
But of course Shakespeare's prophetic insight was far greater
than the selection of a single character would indicate. Through
him, far more than through anyone or anything else, we have
formed, often without knowing it, that humanistic philosophy
which is the basis of our thought, and which holds that the only
true assessment of man's worth must be made through his own
experience as he finds it for himself in facing his own problems.

What these great figures do on a large scale with a prodigious
success is done on a small scale by all poets worthy of the name.
Any poem that succeeds in being a truly individual, and there-
fore unique, work of art preserves something which is worth
preserving and passes it to the common heritage of man. Po-
etry's concern is with the art of life, with the means by which
we can live more fully and more abundantly. Through its
achievements in each generation it continually extends our im-
aginative consciousness and through this our whole outlook.
Though it may not deal specifically with right and wrong, it
deals with a whole world of values as it discovers them in human
experience. A poetical tradition is much more than a habit of
writing poetry, more than a written record of what men have
thought and felt, more even than a vivid, concentrated aware-
ness of the human scene; it is a living, creative force which en-
larges our outlook, quickens our sensibilities, and by breaking
down our habitual limitations of thought and feeling acts as a
powerful antidote to the specialization and departmentalism
which afflict so much of organized life.

Such a tradition usually works through a single language,
since a poet learns his craft from those who have preceded him

in the use of his own speech. This means that it is usually confined to a single country or geographical area, not merely because such an area is the usual unit for a language but because each country has through its history a set of common experiences which the poet assumes and exploits when he writes for his fellows. Thus, though the rich poetical tradition of Central and South America certainly owes much to Spain, each country has its special, national tradition which inevitably informs its poetry and gives to it an individual character, while beyond this there is an air of the New World which lies outside the scope of Spain but belongs to her former colonies because they are set in a different landscape with different conditions of life. Conversely, a single political unit, which embraces peoples of several languages, is likely to nurture several traditions of poetry which follow their own linguistic habits and may be quite independent of one another. Thus the old Austro-Hungarian Empire did not succeed in producing any poetry representative of its whole domains, but produced instead a variety of schools and traditions in German, Hungarian, Czech, and the different branches of South Slavonic. If there is some resemblance between the romantic poetry of the German Austrians and the Czechs, neither has much in common with the heroic lays of the Serbs or even with the powerful, passionate poetry of the Magyars. What matters most is the individual tradition in which a poet works. This is indeed largely determined by local circumstances but is in the main preserved and continued by the literary qualities of a language and the uses to which earlier generations have put them.

A poetical tradition which moves on such lines throws more illumination on the true nature of a people than any record of its external history. At the least, a study of it will confirm and clarify what we already know superificially but do not understand from the inside. The elegance and order of French life reach a new distinction in French verse; the vast metaphysics of Germany have a counterpart in a poetry which relies much upon *Sehnsucht* and is often in search of a *Jenseits;* the deeply rooted individualism of the Chinese permeates a poetry which has a special delicacy and subtlety in treatment of personal relations; the style and variety of Spanish life sustain a poetry remarkable for its dignity and its passion. In such cases poetry may do no more than confirm what we know already, but it makes us look at it in a different way. Something which we have seen from outside reveals its inner nature and the springs of its behavior. Instead of considering abstractions we see concrete examples, which by their vivid appeal convey much more than any general ideas can. The best clue to the understanding of a nation's character is in its poetry, since this reflects what it has treasured from experience and thinks worth preserving.

The importance of such a study becomes more manifest when a national poetry presents a marked contrast with preconceived ideas of the national character. Such ideas are by no means to be dismissed as foolish prejudices; they are usually based on a knowledge of facts. But they are not based on all the facts, and poetry provides a salutary corrective to them. It is, for instance, a startling paradox that England, the nation of shopkeepers and of sturdy common sense, well known for its love of sport and its love of business, suspected of an innate Philistinism, and condemned for too great attention to solid comfort, has maintained an unbroken tradition of poetry since the fourteenth century. Nor is this poetry such as we might expect from a people of merchant adventurers and colonial captains. It is intimate and solitary, tender and delicate. It is not even, as it might well be, insular. It is always ready to learn from abroad and to adapt continental inventions to the native idiom. Nor does the notorious English love of convention hamper it. It is indeed governed by rules, which are part of its admirable style, but it is uncommonly generous in its understanding and its sympathies. A man who had studied English history and then turned to English poetry would certainly be greatly surprised by what he found, and would have to admit that here was something which altered his whole conception of the English character.

Another paradox can be seen in ancient Athens. Perhaps we see it too much through its literature to perceive the appearance it must have presented to other Greek cities. The Athenians were the most ebullient, reckless, adventurous of peoples, always making experiments or trying to impose their will on others or to win everlasting fame through some prodigious exploit, even if it meant incurring universal hatred. Yet in their poetry they proclaimed and dramatized the all-importance of moderation and the Mean. With all their insatiable appetite for life, they would suddenly say that man is but a shadow in a dream and all his desires are dust. This was no mere insurance against the wrath of incalculable gods, no mere conventional tribute to some dim or guilty respect for order. It was part of the Athenian nature and provided the background against which they played their proud and reckless parts. If Athenian tragedy was born from this quarrel with themselves and reflected it in the presentation of superhuman characters coming to appalling dooms, it is also the best means by which we can understand what these men were when they were alive, what swift currents ran in their blood and how, even if dimly and halfheartedly, they tried to control them.

Though a poetical tradition is essentially national and derives much of its strength from being so, it may at times become international and perform a task between peoples. Sometimes the art of one country will spread its influence abroad and through translation and adaptation touch thousands of people whose way of life is alien to it, but who none the less assimilate it and find their outlook changed because the new art appeals to something in themselves which they have not hitherto recognized, or opens up new and attractive fields of sensibility. In Asia, Persia was for some centuries the center of such an influence, which spread not only to the Moslem and Hindu peoples of India but to distant mountaineers and pastoral nomads in Georgia, Armenia, and Bactria. In Europe more than one country has played such a role. The rebirth of lyrical poetry in the twelfth century was largely the work of Provence. A highly specialized poetry born in the courts of Languedoc and Aquitaine spread its power to Northern France, Germany, Portugal, Sicily, Italy, and England. The local poets took up the Provençal themes and measures and adapted them to their own tongues. But though there is a real community both of technique and spirit between the songs of Guillaume of Aquitaine and such poems as the English "Alison," or the Portuguese "Leonoreta," or the dawn-songs and spring-songs of Heinrich von Morungen and Walther von der Vogelweide, this is no case of imitation or of mere adaptation to the local idiom. In each case the Provençal seed falls on a rich, almost prepared ground, in which an indigenous tradition of song has taught men what poetry is and made them ready to accept new forms. The schools of poetry gain a new strength from abroad but lose little of their local color in doing so.

What Provence did for the Middle Ages, Italy did for the Renaissance, Germany and England for the Romantic Age, and France for the end of the nineteenth century. In the sixteenth century France, England, Spain, and Portugal looked to Italy both for their verse forms and for their main subjects, but in each country we forget the Italian models when we read this lively and varied poetry of the emotions. In the Romantic Age, first Goethe and then Byron carried their own kinds of poetry across Europe, until there is little in France or Russia or Spain which cannot be connected with one or the other of them. In the Nineties the French Symbolists and especially Mallarmé evoked a new vision of pure poetry which passed to young poets everywhere and inspired a generation of sublime achievement. Of course, in most of these cases such extensive changes would not have taken place if they had not been initiated by men of remarkable originality, but these men would never have had so great an influence if they had not appealed to something which lay hidden in most European countries and responded vigorously to new methods for its expression. In such situations national and European influences combine to produce a notable result. But this itself suggests that divisions between countries hide great similarities between men and that it is the task of the arts to ignore the divisions and explore the similarities. Though poetry cannot ever be so international as music or painting, it can exert a powerful influence in making men of different countries conscious that they have much to learn from one another because after all they are fashioned from the same clay and inspired by the same breath of life. Any system of politics which denounces internationalism in the arts as a heresy is bound in the end to impoverish its own poetry and to lose much which any wise system of government ought to welcome.

The study of poetry is an important element in the study of civilization, just as the writing of poetry is itself a great civilizing force. In such study we should not underrate the value of two techniques which may not look very important but are indispensable. First, translation. Though it can never be a wholly adequate substitute for the original words, it is nevertheless a potent influence in spreading new outlooks and ideas, in showing to one people what kind of poetry is written by another and suggesting what may be gained by an exploitation of new techniques. The poetry of ancient Rome may almost be said to have begun its mature life when Livius Andronicus translated the *Odyssey* from Greek into Latin and showed how poetry could tell a complex story on a large scale. To a people accustomed to little else than short lays about the doings of their ancestors this was indeed a revelation, and it started the series of epics which is one of the glories of Roman literature. Less obvious but no less powerful is the influence which Shakespeare has had in countries not his own. The translations of his poetry into German and Russian are indeed works of pure poetry, and the result has been his acclimatization in Germany and Russia, whereas in France and Italy, where he has been far less fortunate in his translations, his popularity and influence have been correspondingly less. Our own century has realized the use of translations and benefits greatly from them. Much, for instance, of the modern approach to Chinese civilization has been determined by gifted men who have conveyed in their own tongue the charm and grace of Chinese poetry. Its form is indeed almost impossible to reproduce in any polysyllabic language like English or French, but its matter, at once so different from that of our own poetry and yet so friendly and ultimately so familiar, has passed into our experience and touched not only our poetry but our lives.

A second important instrument is the anthology, especially if it is truly representative of some national tradition of poetry. It provides the right means to start the study of such a tradition, since through it we form some idea of the complex and yet somehow homogeneous experience which has gone into the making of a nation. This is equally true of a tradition which is old and rich like English or Italian, or relatively modern like those of the Americas. In either case the unfolding panorama of poetry reveals to us what a nation has seen and felt through the vicissitudes of its history and what characteristics it has developed. Such a picture cannot fail to excite our curiosity and engage our attention as we see a civilization growing in variety and responding to new challenges. As we do this, we can hardly fail to enjoy not merely a historical spectacle but chapters of spiritual experience which have their own special color but are none the less related to much that we know in ourselves. So with a country like Mexico, which is an unfamiliar terrain for most Europeans and, indeed, for many North Americans, we see how in the New World there has grown a vivid and varied culture which is indeed both Mexican and Central American but is also of our own kin and kind. Just because it is in some respects different from our own, this culture, by exciting our interest in it, enables us at the same time to shift our familiar point of view and to look at our own tradition with fresh eyes. And that, after all, is what anyone desires who believes that the art of life is to be as alive as possible and that for this task poetry is an indispensable means of refreshment and renewal.

C. M. BOWRA

Introduction to the History of Mexican Poetry

Spain: the word glows red and gold, black and purple, a romantic word. Torn between extremes, at once Carthaginian and Roman, Catholic and Mohammedan, medieval and Renaissance, hardly any of the terms normally employed to distinguish the various stages of European history can be satisfactorily applied to the development of Spain. In fact, it is not possible to speak of its "development," because its history is a succession of sudden ups and downs, now a dance and now a lethargy. It is therefore not surprising that the existence of a Spanish Renaissance has been denied. Indeed, at the time when the revolutionary changes of the Renaissance were spreading out of Italy and laying the foundations of the modern world, Spain shut itself off from other countries and withdrew into itself; but not before it had first capitulated to the very spirit which it was later to oppose with a fervor as passionate as its original surrender. It was just at this moment of seduction, when it was imbibing the literature, art, and philosophy of the Renaissance, that Spain discovered America. And hardly had the Spaniard set foot on American soil before he transplanted thither the art and poetry of the Renaissance. They constitute our oldest and most genuine tradition. We Spanish-speaking Americans were born at a moment when Spanish thought had taken on a "universal" complexion. One Mexican writer, Jorge Cuesta, therefore maintains that the most striking feature of our tradition is *deracination*. This is true. The Spain which discovered Mexico was not the Spain of the Middle Ages but the Spain of the Renaissance; and the poetry which the first Mexican poets regarded as their own was the poetry which, in Spain, was thought un-Spanish and alien, i.e., Italian. Our only tradition is heresy toward the Spanish tradition.

Following the Conquest, the Creole writers imitated the Spanish poets who were most divorced from their own soil, sons not only of Spain but of their time. When Menéndez y Pelayo states that "the earliest American poetry may be regarded as an offshoot or continuation of the school of Seville," might we not take his words still further, and claim that the Seville school itself is a branch of the Italian tree? Placed on the periphery of the Spanish sphere, confronted with a world of anonymous ruins and a countryside likewise unnamed, the first Mexican poets tried to overcome the extreme remoteness of their situation by resorting to a universal form of expression which would make them the contemporaries if not the compatriots of their masters in the Peninsula and their Italian models. Such of their works as remain show no trace of the hesitations and excesses of a language in course of formation, which, as it develops, creates a literature and shapes a character. Masters of a "translucent" style, they move effortlessly in a world of ready-made images. Francisco de Terrazas, the first considerable poet of the sixteenth century, represents not dawn but noonday.

The only thing in fact which distinguishes the poetry of Mexico from that of Spain at this time is the absence or scarcity of medieval features. Our poetry is universal in its origins, as in its ideals. Born at a time when the language had reached maturity, it had its source in the Spanish Renaissance. Fathered by Garcilaso, Herrera, and Góngora, it never knew heroic babblings, popular naïveté, realism, or myths. Unlike all other modern literatures, that of Mexico did not move from the regional to the national plane and thence to the universal, but traveled in the opposite direction. The infancy of our poetry corresponded with the high noon of Spanish poetry, to which it belongs by language and from which, for centuries, it differed only in a constant inclination to prefer the universal to the national, the intellectual to the racial.

The abstract and lucid style of the first neo-Spanish poets did not allow the intrusion into their work of the American scene. It was baroque that opened the door to the countryside, the flora and fauna, and the Indian himself. In almost all the baroque poets may be observed a conscious use of the native world. But, by its very exoticism, this merely tended to accentuate the value of the eccentricity looked for in the art of the period. The baroque school could not afford to ignore the aesthetic effects produced by all these materials almost in the raw. Góngora's "Mexican clad in feathers" was taken up by many others. The poets of the seventeenth century, like the Romantics, discovered Nature in America through their European masters. Their references to their natural surroundings were the fruit of aesthetic doctrine and not of personal intuition.

The work of Bernardo de Balbuena has been regarded as marking the birth of American nature poetry. Yet this learned and colorful poet is less concerned to put into words the splendor of the new landscape than to play with his own fancy. Between his eyes and the world around him, the aesthetic doctrine of his time hung a veil. His long poems lack structure because they are not sustained by true poetic imagination, which is always a creator of myths. But his inexhaustible fantasy, his love of full-bodied, resonant words, and the very wealth of their flow, are very American and justify Pedro Henríquez Ureña's opinion that "Balbuena represents America's contribution to the magnificent climax of baroque poetry . . . his baroque is not a complication of ideas, as with the Castilian poets, nor a complication of poetic images, as with the Andalusians, but a profusion of ornament combined with a clear construction of both ideas and images, like the baroque altars in Mexican churches." There it is: the originality of Balbuena is to be sought in the history of styles, rather than in a natural, unhistorical evolution. He himself has left us an excellent definition of his art:

"Si la escultura y el pincel consuelan
con sus primores los curiosos ojos
y en contrahacer el mundo se desvelan. . . ."*

Baroque art is not an imitation of nature, but neither is it pure invention. It aims not at reproducing or at creating the world, but at counterfeiting it, recreating it, and, so far as Balbuena is concerned, exaggerating it, transforming it into a swift and sumptuous game, rich in content and eloquence.

The poetry of the Colonial period, like all derivative art, tends to exaggerate what it copies. In this tendency to go to extremes it is not difficult to detect a desire for singularity. But this exaggerated "Spanishness" was one way of expressing our diffidence in the presence of Spanish art, itself trenchant and given to excess. The other way was by reticence, as exemplified in the work of Juan Ruiz de Alarcón. This great dramatist— and indifferent lyric poet—has given us, in contrast to the plays of Lope de Vega and their dazzling facility, work in which it is not unreasonable to hear an echo of Plautus and Terence. As opposed to Lope and Tirso de Molina, the Mexican playwright depicts human beings rather than situations, a world of reason and balance—above all, a world of reasonable probabilities, in contrast to the impossible reasoning of his rivals. The restraint of Alarcón emphasizes the true meaning of the exaggerations of poets like Bernardo de Balbuena. The nascent literature of Mexico gained ground, at times as a curb on "Spanishness," at others as an intensification of it. In either case it represented the diffidence of a national genius not yet venturing to be itself, oscillating between two extremes.

Religion was the pivot of society and the true spiritual food of its component parts. But religion was on the defensive, seated firmly on its dogmas, for the apogee of Catholicism in America coincided with its decadence in Europe. The religious life of the colony lacked mystical impulse and theological daring. But although it is hard to find figures comparable to San Juan de la

---

* "So sculpture and painting console by their beauty the curious eye, and in counterfeiting the world are ever vigilant. . . ."

Cruz or Fray Luis de León, religious writers of merit abound. Conspicious among them is Fray Miguel de Guevara, author of a number of sacred sonnets, including the famous: "No me mueve mi Dios, para quererte. . . ." As in the case of some other Spanish masterpieces, it is impossible to state that this sonnet was really written by Guevara. In the opinion of Alfonso Méndez Plancarte it is more than probable that it was: the fact that it is written in his own hand certainly suggests this. Other sonnets, this able critic adds, will bear comparison with the poem just mentioned, "especially the one beginning: 'Poner al Hijo en cruz, abierto el seno. . . .' which recalls the most profound of Góngora's sacred sonnets, and surpasses them in emotional power and even in imaginative force." These few poems suffice to place Guevara among the foremost religious poets in the language.

The curiosity which the Indian past excites should not always be regarded as a mere thirst for the exotic. During the seventeenth century many minds were occupied with the problem of how a colonial order could assimilate the native world. The ancient history of the Indians, their myths, their dances, and their crafts, even their religion, formed a secret and inaccessible universe. At the same time, the old beliefs were mingling with the new, and the remnants of the native culture posed questions to which there was no answer. The Virgin of Guadalupe was also Tonantzin, the coming of the Spaniards was confused with the return of Quetzalcoatl, and the ancient native rituals revealed disturbing analogies with those of the Catholic Church. If certain presages of the coming of Christ were to be found in the pagan faith of the Mediterranean, why should they not be encountered also in the history of ancient Mexico? The Conquest was no longer regarded as an event brought about by the will of Spain alone, but as an occurrence for which the Indians had been waiting, and which had been prophesied by their kings and priests. By dint of such interpretations a supernatural link was established between the ancient religions and Catholicism. The Virgin of Guadalupe, ancient goddess of fertility, on whom so many ideas and psychic forces were focused, became the meeting place of the two worlds and the center of Mexican religious life. Her image embodied the reconciliation of the two conflicting worlds, and at the same time expressed the originality of the nation that was coming to birth. Through the Virgin of Guadalupe, Mexico claims to be heir to two traditions. Baroque colonial art exploited this situation, mixed the Indian with the Spanish tradition, and produced a new form of exoticism. A peculiar form of baroque, which might be labeled "guadalupan," was to become the pre-eminent style of New Spain.

Among the poems dedicated to the Virgin, one by Luis de Sandoval y Zapata is outstanding. Every single line of this sonnet "Alada eternidad del viento" contains a memorable image. Better than anyone else, Zapata represents the apogee of baroque art and perfectly expresses the *ingenio* of the period, a form of wit comparable to the conceits of the English metaphysical poets. We know very little of his work which was neglected for centuries and discounted by a literary criticism as unenterprising as it was blind to the qualities of baroque. The fragments of Zapata's work which have been rescued show that he was a man of grave and subtle talent, brilliant and ingenious, the personal heir of both Góngora and Quevedo. From every one of his poems may be quoted lines that are perfect, not so lifelessly faultless in form as terse or sparkling, weighty or winged, and always inevitable. His taste for the unusual image and his love of geometric patterns of thought led him to build delicate musical cages for those birds of the intellect. It is thus possible not only to extract from the few poems remaining to us strange and glittering fragments, but also to come upon two or three sonnets which still form a living whole—solitary towers amid the ruins of his work.

Sor Juana Inés de la Cruz—or, by her real name, Juana de Asbaje—is the noblest figure in the colonial poetry of Spanish America and one of the richest and most profound in our literature. She was beset by critics, biographers, and apologists, but nothing which has been said about her since the seventeenth century is more apt and penetrating than what she herself tells us in her "Respuesta a Sor Filotea de la Cruz." In this letter is to be found the tale of her intellectual vocation; a defense, sometimes ironical, of her thirst for knowledge; the story of her struggle and triumphs; and a criticism of her poetry and also of her critics. These pages reveal Sor Juana as an intellectual, that is to say, a creature for whom life is an exercise of the mind. She wanted to understand everything. Where a religious soul would have found proof of the presence of God, she saw an occasion for hypothesis and questioning. For her, the world was more an enigma than a place for salvation. Symbol of maturity though she is, the Mexican nun is also the image of a society on the verge of schism. A nun by intellectual vocation, she preferred the tyranny of the cloister to that of the world, and for years maintained a precarious balance in a daily conflict between her religious duty and her intellectual curiosity. Defeated, she lapsed into silence, but her silence was that of the intellectual, not that of the mystic.

The poetical works of Sor Juana are numerous, varied, and unequal. The innumerable poems she wrote to order bear witness to her graceful ease and also to her carelessness. But most of her work is saved from this defect, both by its admirable rhetorical construction and by the truths it expresses. Although she said that the only thing she enjoyed writing was "a trifle called 'The Dream,' " her sonnets, *liras*, and *endechas* are the works of a great poet of earthly love. For this witty, passionate, and ironical woman, the sonnet became a natural form of expression. In its luminous dialectic of metaphor—thesis and antithesis—she is consumed and delivered, escapes and surrenders. Less ardent than Louise Labbé, and also less direct, the Mexican poetess goes deeper, and is freer and more daring in her reticences, as well as more mistress of herself in her transports. She uses her intellect not to restrain her passion but to intensify it, and to make it more freely and intentionally inevitable. In its best moments, the poetry of Sor Juana is something more than a sentimental confession or a happy exercise in baroque rhetoric. And even when she is obviously jesting, as in the disquieting portrait of the Countess of Paredes, her sensuality and love of the body give life to the erudite allusions and conceits, which are transformed into a labyrinth of crystal and fire.

"Primero Sueño" ("First Dream") is Sor Juana's most ambitious poem. Although it was a confessed imitation of the "Soledades" of Góngora, the profound difference between the two works is greater than their external similarity. Sor Juana tries to pierce reality, not to make of it a gleaming surface. The vision which we are shown in "Primero Sueño" is a dream of universal night where man and the universe dream and are themselves figments of a dream: a dream of knowledge, a dream of being. Nothing could be further removed from the amorous night of the mystic than this intellectual night, a night of sleepless eyes and sleepless clocks. In the "Soledades," says Alfonso Reyes, Góngora sees man "as an inert mass in the nocturnal landscape." Sor Juana "approaches the sleeper like a vampire, enters into him and his nightmare, looking for a synthesis of wakefulness, drowsing and dream." The substance of the poem is unprecedented in Spanish poetry, and had no influence until quite recent times. "Primero Sueño" is a poem of the intelligence, its ambitions and defeat. It is intellectual poetry, poetry of disenchantment. Sor Juana brings to an end the golden dream of the viceregal period.

Although baroque was prolonged until the middle of the century, the eighteenth century was mainly an epoch of prose. Periodicals were published for the first time; criticism and learning prospered; science, history, and philosophy flourished at the expense of the creative arts. Neither the style of the preceding century nor the new tendency toward neoclassicism produced any writers of importance. The most notable poets of the period wrote in Latin. In the meantime, the ideas of the Enlightenment were awakening a somnolent world. The Revolution of Independence was in the air. The artistic sterility of neoclassicism contrasted with the intellectual fervor of the best minds. At the end of the century a considerable poet appeared: Manuel de Navarrete, a follower of Meléndez Valdés. In his poems, neoclassicism and its shepherds are enveloped in a vague mist of sentimentality, heralding the romantic movement.

The nineteenth century was a period of internal strife and foreign wars. The nation suffered two foreign invasions and a long civil war, ending in the victory of the Liberal Party. The Mexican intelligentsia took part both in politics and in the fighting. To defend their country, shape it, almost—one might say— to invent it, was the task which absorbed Ignacio Ramírez, Guillermo Prieto, Ignacio Manuel Altamirano, and many others. In this exalted atmosphere, the romantic movement began to make its presence felt. The poets wrote. They wrote incessantly, but above all they fought, also without respite. The admiration which their ardent and dramatic lives arouses in us—Acuña committed suicide at twenty-four, Flores died blind and destitute—does not prevent us from recognizing their weaknesses and shortcomings. None of them—with the possible exception of Flores, who, though he had vision, lacked originality of expression—realized what romanticism actually meant. So they dragged out its most superficial features, and abandoned themselves to an eloquent, sentimental form of writing, false in its skin-deep sincerity and poor even in its magniloquence. The world's irrationality, the dialogue between the individual and the world, the fullness of power conferred by dreams and by love, the yearning for a lost unity, the prophetic power of the word, and lastly, the practice of poetry as apprehending, through loving, reality—that universe of hidden affinities rediscovered by romanticism—these things were neither evident nor of interest to most of the poets of this period. They move in the realm of sentiment, and delight in telling us of their loves and enthusiasms, but they have hardly anything of that sense of the sacred peculiar to all genuine romantic art. The greatness of these writers is to be found in their lives, which were consecrated to the defense of liberty.

The survival of neoclassicism in this atmosphere of change and revolution is remarkable. Almost always strict versifiers, the academic poets preserved the language of romantic excesses.

None of them is a genuine poet, but José Joaquín Pesado and Joaquín Arcadio Pagaza contrive a discreet re-creation of the Mexican landscape. Their influence and example were to be of profit to Manuel José Othón. The stoicism of Ignacio Ramírez, perhaps the most representative mind of the age, found dignified expression in a few scornful triplets. Altamirano, the leader of the younger generation, tried to reconcile the conflicting trends and initiated a timid literary nationalism, which produced no offspring of note.

Manuel José Othón is an inheritor of the academic tradition. There is no attempt at innovation in his work. If he shunned romanticism, he showed as little taste for the "modernistic" rhetoric which was carrying all before it at the end of his life. Much of his work is indeed indistinguishable in theme and intention from that of Pagaza, a poet to whom he is related not only by a community of taste but also by a similar aesthetic outlook. But the sonnets of the "Idilio Salvaje," (Wild Idyll)—"A una estepa del Nazas" and a few others—represent something more than the "poetry of nature" in which the academic school liked to ossify itself. The desert of the north, "the dry basin of a dead ocean," with its high, cruel sky, ceased to be a spectacle and a symbol. It became the mirror of the poet's exhausted being, and the aridity of love and the final sterility of passion were reflected in the nakedness of the savannah. Beneath the traditional form and language glitters the unblinking eye of a Nature which can be sated only by annihilating what it loves, and has no other purpose than to consume and be consumed. A fierce high-region sun scorches the rocks of the desert, the image of his own self in ruins. The solitude of man is one of the rhymes in the manifold solitude of Nature. The sonnet plumbs a new depth and its echoes and parallels are an allusion to another inexorable geometry, and to other, more deadly and hollow rhymes.

Whereas Othón was an academic poet who discovered romanticism and thus escaped the parnassianism of his school, Salvador Díaz Mirón took the opposite direction: he is a romantic who aspires to classicism. The poetry of his first period shows traces of Victor Hugo at his most eloquent, and the vigor of Byron. After a silence lasting several years he published *Lascas,* the only book which he acknowledged as entirely his own. The title of this work describes his poetry, or more precisely, moments of poetry wrested in his anger and impatience from a style which is always a curb. *Lascas,* chips of stone from shooting stars, brief flashes lighting for a moment a dark and arrogant soul. The parnassian Díaz Mirón did not reject romanticism; he subdued it, but he never succeeded in taming it. And from this struggle—which sometimes took the form of a barren mastery and distortion of the language—spring tense lines—"like the silence of the star above the tumult of the waves."

In contrast to the colorless language of the poets who had preceded him, and in contrast likewise to the gewgaws of almost all the modernists, the poetry of Díaz Mirón is as hard and brilliant as a diamond: a diamond whose fires sparkle not too dimly but too brightly. He was a poet who wanted only to master his material, but he never found a style that could express his thought without stifling it. At the end of this breathless contest, his work resolved into silence. Silence is the form peculiar to him, the final mould of his mind. Or, as Jorge Cuesta has said, "his fecundity is in his silence. Other poets were unworthy to keep silent." As the precursor and master of modernism, Díaz Mirón's adventure was above all a verbal adventure. But this adventure was also a drama—a drama of pride. For this craftsman was the first Mexican poet to show an awareness of evil and its dreadful creative powers.

Modernism is not merely the assimilation of parnassian and symbolist poetry. In discovering French poetry, Spanish-American modernism also discovered the Spanish classics, forgotten or betrayed in Spain. Above all, it created a new language which became the vehicle, in an extremely fertile period, of some great poets: Rubén Darío, Leopoldo Lugones, Julio Herrera y Reissig. In Mexico, modernism might have found a greater depth of expression if the Mexicans had realized the true significance of the new trend. Modernism took the form of indifference toward Spanish traditionalism; it is, indeed, impossible not to regard it as the heir of the tradition which founded Mexico. For the rest of Spanish America it opened the doors of the universal poetic tradition; to the Mexicans, on the other hand, it gave an opportunity to renew their own tradition. Every revolution possesses or creates a tradition. Darío and Lugones invented their own. Gutiérrez Nájera and Amado Nervo never knew that they had one, and that is why the meaning of the modernist revolution escaped them. The modernism of these two poets is nearly always exoticism, that is to say, they were constantly re-creating themselves in the most decorative and superficial elements of the new style.

Despite his limitations, Manuel Gutiérrez Nájera reveals at isolated moments, in some of his poems, that other world, that other reality, which is the vision of every true poet. Sensitive and elegant, when he is not delighting in his tears and discoveries, he attacks with graceful melancholy the theme of the shortness of life. His poetry, as he said himself in one of his most quoted poems, "will not completely die." In his modernist period, Amado Nervo manipulates, without taste but with freshness and authenticity, the stock-in-trade of symbolism. Later, he decided to do without it. In fact, he simply executed a change of garment; the symbolist garb, which suited him, was discarded for the mantle of the religious and moral philosopher. Poetry lost by the change, but neither religion nor ethics gained anything.

Other poets, less applauded in their day, approached nearer to the magic of poetry. Francisco A. de Icaza, bitter and sober, attained in his short poems a terseness which was both concentrated and lyrical. Luis G. Urbina continued for the most part along the sentimental lines of Nájera, but was saved by a temperament akin to that of an impressionist painter. His best work, made up of twilights and seascapes, reveals him as a worthy heir of the landscape tradition. With less intensity than Othón, but with more imagination and subtlety, Urbina achieves a delicate balance of expression. It is significant that these two Mexican poets escape from the falsity of modernism by resorting to a universal tradition. Mexican poetry did not find its native form; every time that it dared to express its best and most secret self, it had no option but to make use of a culture that was its own only by an act of intellectual conquest.

In contrast to the modernist poets, who borrowed from the parnassians and symbolists only the most perishable elements, Enrique González Martínez shows a deeper and more thoughtful sensibility, and an intelligence which dares to question the dark face of the world. The austerity of González Martínez, the absence of almost every unpredictable element—which is the salt of poetry—and the didacticism of some of his work have led to his being regarded as the first Spanish-American poet to break with the modernist movement. He was an owl confronting a swan. But in fact, González Martínez was not opposed to modernism; he stripped it and laid it bare. In depriving it of its sentimental and parnassian trappings, he redeemed it, made it aware of itself and of its hidden meaning. González Martínez confers upon modernism a Mexican originality, that is to say, he gives it consciousness and links it to a tradition. He is not therefore a denier of modernism, but the only truly modernist poet Mexico has had—in the sense that Darío and Lugones in America, Machado and Jiménez in Spain were modernists. The attention he devoted to landscape, above all the night landscape, brought about a change of influence; the dialogue between man and his surroundings was resumed. Poetry ceased to be a description or a complaint and became a spiritual adventure. After González Martínez, parnassian rhetoric, romantic sentimentalism, and the flashiness of the minor modernists became impossible. Once he had endowed modernism with a conscience, the poet's attitude toward poetry underwent a change, although he left the language and its symbols unaltered. His importance lies, not in his hostility to the modernist style— which he never abandoned—but in the fact that he was the first to give poetry a sense of the *gravity* of words. His work brings to an end the period opened by two other solitaries: Othón and Díaz Mirón.

One of the first books of poems published by Alfonso Reyes was called *Pausa*. This title not only is a key to his poetry but also places it in relation to that of his immediate predecessors and followers. Reyes was never a modernist. From the outset, his work stood apart from the movement. With his eager yet firmly rooted mind, as much of the air as of the earth, Reyes peeped into the hidden source of many a stream, suffered manifold temptations, and never said: "Of this water I will not drink." Everyday speech, colloquial turns of phrase, the monologue of Mallarmé, the Greek chorus, and the Spanish of the golden age all meet in his work. He is a traveler in several languages and an explorer of many different worlds, closely resembling Valéry Larbaud in the catholicity of his curiosity and of his experiences—sometimes real expeditions of conquest into lands hitherto unknown. He mixes reading with life, reality with dream, dancing with walking, erudition with the freshest invention. In his work, prose and verse, criticism and creation, permeate and influence one another. Therefore it is not possible to limit his poetry to his verse: his longest poem, and perhaps his most beautiful and profound, is a huge fresco in prose: *Visión de Anáhuac,* a reconstruction of the life and landscape of Mexico before the conquest. Nor would it be fair to overlook various translations of his, veritable re-creations, among which must be mentioned two names that are poles apart: Homer and Mallarmé. It is said that Alfonso Reyes is one of the best prose writers in the language. Let us add that this prose would not be what it is if it were not the prose of a poet.

José Juan Tablada and Ramón López Velarde openly and ostentatiously broke with modernism. The former was a deserter from that movement. The poetry of his youth is a typical example of the brilliant and shallow products of the modernist school. But Tablada, curious, passionate, never looking back, his feet winged, heard the grass growing and scented the new beast before anyone else—the magnificent, ferocious beast which was to devour so many slumberers: poetic imagery. Having fallen in love with Japanese poetry, he introduced the *haiku* into our language shortly before, so he tells us, the fashion spread to France. His bestiary shows a penetrating understanding of the animal world, and his monkeys, parrots, and armadillos gaze upon us with steady, bright eyes. Like a miniature sun Tablada's *haiku* is hardly ever a separate image, taken from a longer poem, but a fixed and twinkling star, immovable in appearance only, since it is always revolving on its own axis. The *haiku* could easily be assimilated to the popular *copla,* which explains its extraordinary vogue. Many adopted it in America, and in Spain Juan Ramón Jiménez and Machado wrote some of their best "maxims and epigrams" in poems of three or four lines, which, if they echo Andalusian poetry, also recall this Oriental verse form.

No sooner was the *haiku* accepted as a regular form than Tablada abandoned it and began to write his "ideographical" poems. His experiment, though perhaps showing less genius, was not unlike Apollinaire's, who was then publishing his "Calligrammes." The typography of poetry distracted him only for a moment. Always smiling and always in a hurry, he spent a few years touring the entire world of poetry. Finally he returned to his own country and published a series of "Mexican" poems, which cannot be regarded as mere imitations of those published a short time previously by López Velarde, although they show his influence and follow his example. Less profound than Velarde, and less personal, Tablada has a livelier and more colorful vision. His style, almost entirely free of modernistic ornaments, is flexible, ironical, light, and gay. He gives us a Mexico of ballets and country fairs, fireworks and shouting. In his poems we find, alive for the first time, our sacred and domestic animals, the idols, the old religions, and the art of the ancients. López Velarde never knew that world. Fascinated by the life-and-death struggle between the provinces and the capital, his gaze never wandered from the Mexico of the Creole and the mestizo, at once popular and refined, Catholic even when it was Jacobin. Tablada's view is broader. Occultist and traveler, he looked at his country with different eyes and took as his own the exoticism of its gods and of its colors. He was one of the first to realize the wealth of our native heritage and the importance of its visual arts. In contrast with López Velarde, Tablada's style is invented rather than created, premeditated rather than inevitable. But he is also livelier and more vigorous; he is more playful, too—he knows how to smile and laugh; he flies, and falls, more frequently. In a word, he is more daring.

In spite of the differences which separate them, one thing binds these two poets together: their love of the unusual image and their shared belief in the value of surprise. That is why Tablada was one of the first to discover López Velarde and why, years later, he was quite ready to acknowledge his debt to the poet of Zacatecas. Whereas Tablada was a visual poet, capable of seizing a moment's reality in three lines, the other was a slow-thinking man, constantly carrying on a dialogue with himself. He did not use his imagination to light fireworks, but to delve deeper into himself and to express with the utmost truth what he had to say: "I long to eject every syllable that is not born of the combustion of my bones." López Velarde was a poet by destiny.

Like all true poets, he was preoccupied with language. He wanted to have one of his own. But he desired to create a personal language because he had something intensely personal to say; something to say to us and something to say to himself, which, until he had said it, would give him no rest. His sensitiveness to words is all the keener for his profound awareness of himself and of his own conflict. It should be added that while this awareness led him to invent his own personal language, this in turn drove him in upon himself and revealed to him a part of his being which otherwise would always have remained unexpressed and invisible.

Two events aided López Velarde's discovery of his country and himself. The first was the Mexican Revolution, which broke up a social and cultural order that was a mere historical superstructure—a straitjacket crushing and deforming the nation. In destroying the feudal order, the Revolution tore off the masks which one after another had covered the face of Mexico. The Revolution revealed to López Velarde a "Castilian-Moorish fatherland, with streaks of Aztec," poorer than before but more truly our own. And while the other poets turned their gaze outward, he looked inward and for the first time in our history dared to describe this land without dissimulation and without reducing it to an abstraction. López Velarde's Mexico is a concrete Mexico, the one in which he lived from day to day.

The other decisive event for the poetry of López Velarde was his discovery of the capital. The tide of the Revolution, as much as his own literary ambitions, took him to Mexico City at a time when his mind, but not his taste and his poetry, had matured. His surprise, confusion, delight, and bitterness must have been equally great. In Mexico City he discovered women, loneliness, doubt, and the devil. And as he was enduring these disturbing revelations he was also becoming acquainted with the poems of a few South American poets who had dared to break with modernism by carrying it to extremes. Chief among these were Julio Herrera y Reissig and Leopoldo Lugones. A perusal of the latter's El Lunario Sentimental is indispensable for understanding the sources of López Velarde's poetry. (The influence of Jules Laforgue on the Argentinian poet poses a curious problem: was López Velarde directly acquainted with Laforgue or only through Lugones?) His contact with the works of these poets at once changed his style and outlook. Contemporary critics found him tortuous, incomprehensible, and affected. The truth is quite otherwise; because of his quest for imagery, his almost perfidious use of out-of-the-way adjectives, and his disdain of ready-made forms, his poetry ceased to be a sentimental confession and became the expression of a soul and its anguish.

The discovery of Lugones' poetry would merely have turned López Velarde into a distinguished rhetorician if he had not at the same time remembered the idiom of the region where he was born. His originality consists in this happy combination of the ardent and "opaque" language of central Mexico with the manner of Lugones. Unlike Laforgue, who dropped from "poetic diction" into colloquialisms, and obtained from that shock an unusual brilliance, López Velarde constructs out of everyday and apparently realistic elements a sinuous and intricate sentence which, in its most exalted moments, culminates in a

startling image. This highly personal and inimitable language
enabled him to discover his own inner self and that of his coun-
try. Without it, López Velarde would have been a sentimental
poet: with it alone, a clever rhetorician. His own drama and the
drama of his language turned him into a genuine poet, more,
into the first truly Mexican poet. For with López Velarde begins
Mexican poetry proper, which until then had found no tongue
and had poured itself into forms of expression which it could
call its own only because they were universal.

But apart from the intrinsic value of López Velarde's poetry,
the lesson which he, and to a lesser extent Tablada, provides
for us is that neither poet resorted to forms already tested and
sanctioned by universal tradition, but dared to invent other,
untransmittable forms of their own. In the case of López Vel-
arde, the invention of new forms was combined with a scrupu-
lous respect for the language of his time and of his people, as
with all true innovators. Though some of his poetry may seem
to us naive or limited, nothing can prevent us from seeing in it
something which his followers have not entirely achieved as yet:
the search for the universal through what is genuinely our own.
To follow after López Velarde is not easy; it demands original-
ity and loyalty to our time and to our people, that is to say, it
demands a catholicity that does not betray us and a fidelity
that does not isolate or stifle us. And if it is true that we cannot
return to the poetry of López Velarde, what makes this return
impossible is just that his poetry marks a starting point.

Contemporary Mexican poetry, which has unfortunately had
to be omitted from this anthology, derives from López Velarde's
experience. Its brief story confirms that all poetic activity feeds
upon history, that is to say, upon the language, impulses, myths,
and images of its own time, and likewise it confirms that the
poet tends to dissolve or transcend the mere historical process.
Every poem is an attempt to reconcile history and poetry for
the benefit of poetry. The poet always seeks to elude the tyr-
anny of history even when he identifies himself with the society
in which he lives, and when he participates in what is called
"the current of the age"—an extreme case which is becoming

less and less imaginable in the modern world. All great poetic experiments—from the magic formula and the epic poem to automatic writing—claim to use the poem as a melting-pot for history and poetry, fact and myth, colloquialism and imagery, the date which can never be repeated and the festivity, a date which is alive and endowed with a secret fertility, ever returning to inaugurate a new period. The nature of a poem is analogous to that of a Fiesta which, besides being a date in the calendar, is also a break in the sequence of time and the irruption of a present which periodically returns without yesterday or tomorrow. Every poem is a Fiesta, a precipitate of pure time.

The relationship between men and history is one of slavery and dependence. For if we are the only protagonists of history, we are also its raw material and its victims: it can only be fulfilled at our expense. Poetry radically transforms this relationship; it can only find fulfilment at the expense of history. All its products—the hero, the assassin, the lover, the allegory, the fragmentary inscription, the refraiñ, the oath; the involuntary exclamation on the lips of the child at play, the condemned criminal, the girl making love for the first time; the phrase borne on the wind, the shred of a cry—all these, together with archaism, neologism, and quotation, will never resign themselves to dying, or to being battered against the wall. They are bent on attaining to the end, on existing to the utmost. They extricate themselves from cause and effect. They wait for the poem which will rescue them and make them what they are. There can be no poetry without history, but poetry has no other mission than to transmute history. And therefore the only true revolutionary poetry is apocalyptic poetry.

Poetry is made out of the very substance of history and society—language. But it seeks to re-create language in accordance with laws other than those which govern conversation and logical discourse. This poetic transmutation occurs in the innermost recesses of the language. The phrase—and not the isolated word—is the cell, the simplest element of language. A word cannot exist without other words, a phrase without other phrases.

That is to say, every sentence always contains an implicit reference to another, and is susceptible of explanation by another. Every phrase constitutes a "wish to say" something, referring explicitly to something beyond it. Language is a combination of mobile and interchangeable symbols, each indicating "toward" what it is going. In this way both meaning and communication are based on the "intentionality" of words. But no sooner does poetry touch them than they are changed into rhythmic units or into images; they stand on their own and are sufficient unto themselves. Words suddenly lose their mobility; there are various ways of saying a thing in prose; there is only one in poetry. The poetical word has no substitute. It is not a *wish to say something,* but is something *irrevocably said.* Or alternatively, it is not a "going toward" something, nor a "speaking" of this or that. The poet does not speak of horror or of love: he shows them. Irrevocable and irreplaceable, the words of poetry become inexplicable except in terms of themselves. Their meaning is no longer beyond, but within them; the image is "in" the meaning.

The proper function of the poetic image is to resolve into a unity realities which appear to us conflicting and irreducible. And this operation takes place without removing or sacrificing the conflicts and antagonisms between the entities which it evokes and re-creates. That is why the poetic image is inexplicable in the strict sense of the term. Now poetic language partakes of the ambiguity with which reality reveals itself to us. In transmuting the language, the image not only opens the door to reality, it also, as it were, strips reality bare and shows it to us in its final unity. The phrase becomes an image. The poem is a single image, or an indivisible constellation of images. The void left by the disappearance of what we call reality is peopled with a crowd of heterogeneous or conflicting visions, inevitably seeking to resolve their discord into a solar system of allusions—the poem: a universe of opaque, corruptible words which can yet light up and burn whenever there are lips to touch them. At certain times, in the mouths of some speakers, the phrase-mill becomes a source of evident truths requiring no demonstration. Then we are transported into the fullness of time. By exploiting language to the utmost the poet transcends it. By emphasizing history, he lays it bare and shows it for what it is—time.

When history allows us to suspect that it is perhaps no more than a ghostly procession, without meaning or end, ambiguity of language becomes more marked and prevents any genuine dialogue. Words lose their meaning, and thereby their power to communicate. The degradation of history into a mere sequence of events involves the degradation of language, too, into a collection of lifeless symbols. All men use the same words, but they do not understand one another. And it is useless for men to try to "reach an agreement" on the meanings of words. Language is not a convention, but a dimension from which man cannot be separated. Every verbal adventure is total; a man stakes his whole self and life on a single word. The poet is a man whose very being becomes one with his words. Therefore, only the poet can make possible a new dialogue. The destiny of the poet, particularly in a period such as ours, is "donner un sens plus pur aux mots de la tribu." This implies that words are rooted out of the common language and brought to birth in a poem. What is called hermeticism of modern poetry springs from that fact. But words are inseparable from men. Consequently, poetic activity cannot take place outside the poet, in the magic object represented by the poem; rather does it take man himself as the center of its experience. Opposites are fused in man himself, not in the poem alone. The two are inseparable. The poems of Rimbaud are Rimbaud himself, the adolescent fencing with shining blasphemies, despite all attempts to convert him into a kind of brute upon whom the word descended. No, *the poet and his word are one.* Such has been, during the past hundred years, the motto of the greatest poets of our civilization. Nor has the meaning of that last great movement of the century—surrealism—been any different. The grandeur of these attempts—to which no poet worthy of the name can be indifferent—lies in their endeavor to destroy once and for all, and in desperation, the dualism which tears us asunder. Poetry leaps into the unknown, or it is nothing.

In present circumstances, it may seem ludicrous to refer to the extravagant claims of poetry. Never has the domination of history been greater than now, never has the pressure of "events" been so suffocating. In proportion as the tyranny of "what to do next" becomes more and more intolerable—since our consent has not been asked for the doing, and since it is almost always directed toward man's destruction—so does poetic activity become more secret, isolated, and rare. Only yesterday, to write a poem or to fall in love were subversive activities, compromising the social order by exposing its double character. Today, the very notion of order has disappeared and its place has been taken by a combination of forces, masses, and resistances. Reality has cast aside its disguises and contemporary society is seen for what it is: a heterogeneous collection of things "homogenized" by the whip or by propaganda, directed by groups distinguishable from one another only by their degree of brutality. In these circumstances, poetic creation goes into hiding. If a poem is a Fiesta, it is one held out of season, in unfrequented places—an underground festivity.

But poetic activity is rediscovering all its ancient subversive powers by this very secrecy, impregnated with eroticism and the occult, a challenge to an interdict not less condemnatory for not being explicitly formulated. Poetry, which yesterday was required to breathe the free air of universal communion, continues to be an exorcism for preserving us from the sorcery of force and of numbers. It has been said that poetry is one of the means by which modern man can say *No* to all those powers which, not content with disposing of our lives, also want to rule our consciences. But this negation carries within it a *Yes* which is greater than itself.

OCTAVIO PAZ

Foreword

Every anthology is a compromise. The compiler's freedom of choice is subject to historical, linguistic, or geographical limitations, not to mention those imposed by taste, training, and temperament. It may therefore be advisable to specify the limitations of this book.

In the first place, this volume is an anthology of Mexican poetry written in Spanish. The great esoteric poems of the Maya and the lyrics, epics, and sacred songs of the Plateau, which are almost all written in the Nahuatl language, have of necessity been excluded. There is no need, however, to regret this omission, since I understand that a volume of pre-Columbian poetry is in course of preparation. When it appears I am sure that it will both surprise and fascinate its readers.

The popular poetry of Mexico, the *corridos, canciones,* and other traditional forms derived from those introduced by the Spaniards in the sixteenth century, also finds no place in these pages. To include this popular poetry would have meant doubling the size of the book. Moreover, many of these *corridos* and *canciones* are merely variations of Spanish lays and poems and there seemed no reason to include the former and reject the latter. Both form part of the same current and are, as it were, branches and tributaries of a great water system irrigating all Spanish America. It would be preferable, therefore, to devote a separate volume to Mexican popular and traditional poetry, which is one of the world's richest storehouses of folk songs and legends.

Lastly, living authors have been omitted, except for Alfonso Reyes, without whom the last part of the anthology would have been impaired. Of all the omissions, this is the most regrettable, since the work of the Mexican poets is among the best in modern Spanish poetry.

The anthology covers the period from 1521 to 1910. Within these limits I have been influenced by other and stricter considerations. The first was historical. For it was not simply a question of picking out the poems most in keeping with my own prepossessions, taste, and instinct, but rather of giving adequate representation to each historical period. On the other hand, foreign readers—for whom this book is intended—are not interested in all Mexican poets of merit, but only in the most outstanding. Moreover, the poems are to be translated, and in making my selections I had to bear the translator in mind.

Both in choosing the poems and in writing the introduction, I have consulted the various anthologies and critical studies already published. Among works dealing with the Colonial period, I should mention particularly those of Alfonso Reyes and Alfonso Méndez Plancarte, and among related studies and anthologies those of Marcelino Menéndez y Pelayo, Antonio Castro Leal, Jorge Cuesta, and Manuel Maples Arce.

OCTAVIO PAZ

An Anthology of Mexican Poetry

Francisco de Terrazas (1525?–1600?)

Sonnet

I dreamed that I was thrown from a crag
by one who held my will in servitude,
and all but fallen to the griping jaws
of a wild beast in wait for me below.

In terror, gropingly, I cast around
for wherewith to uphold me with my hands,
and the one closed about a trenchant sword,
and the other twined about a little herb.

Little and little the herb came swift away,
and the sword ever sorer vexed my hand
as I more fiercely clutched its cruel edges. . . .

Oh wretched me, and how from self estranged,
that I rejoice to see me mangled thus
for dread of ending, dying, my distress!

Fernán González de Eslava (*ca.* 1534–*ca.* 1601)

To the Nativity

Evil flees the earth,
now comfort is come:
God is on earth,
now earth is heaven.
Now the world is even
as the eternal Good,
since in the Crib
all heaven is;
all that lacked to the glory
of earth is given:
God is on earth,
now earth is heaven.
Now Man He descends
that ye may rise;
now God and Man
one name unites.
Twixt heaven and earth
now the strife is striven:
God is on earth,
now earth is heaven.

Bernardo de Balbuena (1561 or 1562–1627)

Immortal Springtime and Its Tokens

The bright rays of lofty Phaeton shine
upon the gold of Colchos and restore
to life the frozen and inanimate world.

The jasmine buds, the plants grow green again,
and lovely Flora with her garland sets
upon the heights their crown and ornament.

Amalthea scatters roses from her lap
the limpid air sheds love and merriment,
emerald and hyacinth deck the hills.

All things are redolent of summer, all
distil sweet vapours, all are saturate
with the fresh amber welling in their flowers.

And what though so it is in all the world,
yet in this paradise of Mexico
freshness has set its kingdom and its court.

Mistress, here it seems as though the hand
of heaven had stayed its choice on hanging gardens,
and heaven itself would fain be gardener.

Here May and April flourish all year long
in temperate pleasantness and grateful cool,
their zephyrs soft, their skies serene and bright.

Between the mount of Ossa and a spur
of towering Olympus there is spread
a valley full of freshness and of flowers,

whose beauty Peneus, with his grateless child,
increasingly enriches and augments
with leaves of laurel and with silver streams.

Here the sweet-smelling cyperus abounds,
sung by snowy swans who moist their wings
in the cold crystalline of sleeping meres.

Here midst grass and flower, shade and peace,
trembling waters lap against the sides
of dark caves murmurous with quiet winds.

The waves uprear their spume of pearly spray,
arching above the sand and grainy gold
whereon they break and washing glide away.

White shells re-echo to the plashing stream,
and by yon tangle of aspen, willow and sedge
greeny sea-wrack coils a snaky tress.

Here the hart gambols, there the porcupine,
laden with strawberries and purple-shells,
gives proofs sufficient of his industry.

The bird of Phasis cries, the nightingale,
deep in the tangles of an alder-tree,
sings till the air is steeped in suavity.

To make an end, this human paradise,
so celebrated in Greek eloquence,
with more of wit and elegance than just cause,

is Tempe's spacious vale, by fancy held
to be the cradle of immortal summer,
without an equal, nay without a rival.

Dale most fair I doubt not, but withal
it is as nought, it is as jot and tittle
beside the flowering Mexican domain.

Henceforth its fame is sullied and obscured
increasingly: beside this deathless freshness
its grandeur were a sorry grandeur indeed.

Here midst devious streams the spring
enjoys her treasures in security,
her beauty never to be soiled by time.

She shelters in her kirtle pleasure's romps,
and in pellucid freshets, glassy cold,
perpetuates her mirrored youthfulness.

Here flourishes the laurel, shade and shelter
from all celestial rigour, solemn crown
of aged sages and of poets rare;

and the impetuous almond that proclaims
tidings of summer and, to make them known,
its blossoms jeopardizes and its life;

and the lofty pine exuberant
with pearls of lucent gum, and the vine
proffering its fresh grapes to the thirsty grasp;

brave water-lilies, scenting of jessamine,
and the amorous ivy intertwined
with pretty tendril claws in beech and elm;

the cruel mulberry whose gloomy haunts
embower songs of love, the shady willow,
and the still unconquered Orient palm;

fair ornament of gardens, the funereal
cypress, and the stalwart silver-tree
rearing its bulwark gainst the stormy main;

the glossy box, heavy, hard and trim,
the tamarisk close by the crystal wave,
the brazen oak, the poplar without flaw;

the knotty ilex with its rigid boughs,
the cramoisy and the coral strawberry,
the lofty cedar reaching to the skies;

the grey walnut-tree, the bitter fennel,
and it, befouled by the infernal fumes,
whose leaves enwreathe the brows of Hercules;

the snowy orange-blossom that summer gives
to us in earnest of its bittersweets,
uncertain gage of dubious benefits;

among scarlet poppies the faint gleam
as if of grains of pearl upon the sand,
seen through the taintless water's limpid glass;

the rose half-open and brimful of pearls,
the fresh carnation, bathed in cochineal,
green sweet-basil, vervain and sandal-wood;

the amorous and tender clover-grass,
the ever restless turnsol or marigold,
the tender jasmine, the crimson gillyflower;

the purple violet, the blue flower-de-luce,
the blithesome garden-balm, the pointed thyme,
the bilberry, fresh myrtle and white musk-rose;

flowering rosemary, the best of all
the herbs and flowers that the field could give,
red everlastings and rude calamint;

sweet garden-broom imparting to its haunt
the scent of ambergris, and little pinks,
maidenly, with many-colored flowers;

green ferns and wild churlish camomile,
amorous jonquils, tender fodder-grass,
flowery meadows and sweet-smelling pastures;

bitter cresses, all entanglement,
spangled over with little bells of gold,
scattering their freshness through this pleasant land;

and the Madonna lily that wittingly
I had forgot, sitting between thy brows,
whose whiteness it has borrowed for its own;

hyacinths and daffodils that were given
in earnest of thy coming to the orchards
and to be a promise of flowery boons;

joyous flowers, that in olden times
were monarchs of the world, shepherds and nymphs,
and dwell in bloom because in bloom they ceased;

birds of the air most beautifully hued,
various in plumage, various in song,
skylarks, popinjays and nightingales,

that to the tumult of the wind and wave,
in most suave and sonorous harmony,
temper their unpremeditated strains;

and in the chilly pools above their beds
of shining glass, the nereids interlace
their graceful windings and lascivious coils;

some amid green sedges twine about,
others in the glittering crystal wave
weave and unweave their specious twists and turns.

The limpid waters shimmering far and wide,
troubled like to broken looking-glass,
dazzle the sight with trembling radiance,

and, impearled with blanching foam, reveal,
deep in their vitreous transparencies,
lovely naiads wrought in ivory.

They frolick, gambol, and with joyous starts
wanton on the yielding crystal sheen
in countless figures, miens and attitudes.

One from the mantling wave strikes plumes of spray,
another glides along with sidelong stroke,
others course to and fro, or twist, or roll.

One, whose fairness is unparagoned,
with garlands of alternate gold and flowers
wreathes and embellishes her vaunted grace.

This loveliness, these beauties unconfined,
here dwell and take their pleasure all year long,
exempt from fear and discord and alarums,

in a royal plaisaunce which, in very truth,
exceeds in beauty Cyprus and in balm
of clime and excellence of site the world.

Woods dark with freshness, thickets fresh with shade,
whose immortal verdancy the brushes
of April and of May bedight with flowers.

In fine all things, orchards, gardens, nymphs,
crystal and palm, walnuts, ivy, elms,
pines and poplars, laurels and almond-trees,

trellis and mulberry, cypress, cedar, beech,
box and tamarisk, ilex, oak and fir,
vine and arbutus, fennel and medlar-trees,

orange-blossom, poppies and carnations,
pinks and roses, lilies and irises,
musk and rosemary, sloe and gillyflower,

balm-gentle, clover, vervain, sandal-wood,
myrtle and jessamine, marigold and broom,
bilberry and goldful camomile,

thyme and mead and tangling watercress,
narcissus and sweet-basil and lady-fern,
and as many flowers more as April strows,

here by the supreme giver one and all
in stintless grace and beauty are bestowed.
This is their dwelling, these their native fields,
and this the tide of spring in Mexico.

(fragment of *Grandeza Mexicana*)

Fernando de Córdova y Bocanegra (1565–1589)

Song to the Most Holy Name of Jesus

Divine Name, brief and compendious,
which earth bows down before and heaven adores,
which makes the realm of night to tremble, appalled;
yoke set upon the mocking serpent's neck,
unfathomable ocean sea of virtues,
lettered epitome of endless might:
Divine Name, contrived
by Sapience to embolden
man's dumb and halting tongue:

and if mine own, albeit plain and rude,
partake of thy sweetness in its purposes,
then by thy grace and on propitious wing
its accents unto heaven will ascend.

Divine Name, sweetness, tenderness,
salvation, bounty, life, light, peace,
lettered promise of security;
snow that appeases the lascivious fire,
honey that rids the mouth of bitterness,
salve that brings healing to the mortal wound:
Divine Name, life
that gives life to the dead,
bulwark of man's faith
in the promise, given in the name of God,
that his old forfeiture shall be redeemed;
and, by this name alone,
such credit it commands,
trust dwells among men.

Divine Name, I know no instrument
nor any suavity of harmonious strains
that so uplifts the downcast soul
as the voice uttering
thy sweetness: for there is no heart
so hard but softens to thy tender sound.
Name in truth divine,
for in thy company
my soul makes bold
—when on it soft and loving thus thou stealest—
to stay the pains of hell:
and those in torment thou assuagest not,
because not lovingly,
but rigorously thou strikest on their ears.

Divine Name, no more:
all else were but to offend thee.

The tongue be quiet and the heavens still;
and so, in silence, on the lowly earth
—since mortal speech is powerless to praise thee
in more exalted mode—
the only care of all be to adore thee.

Juan Ruiz de Alarcón (1580 or 1581–1639)

Feast by the Manzanares

Midst the opacous gloom
and dense opacities
that with its elms the grove,
night with its shadows shed,
a table was ensconced,
square and clean and neat,
Italian in device,
Spanish in opulence.
Cloths and serviettes
in countless figures folded
were birds and beasts in all
but animation.
On four sidetables, set
in quadrate symmetry,
stood silver plate and gold,
glasses and earthenware.
Scarce an elm with boughs
in all Sotillo stood,
for they had fallen to raise
the six tents here and there
disposed; four hid from view
four different quires; another,
first courses and desserts,
and the sixth the meats.

My lady came in her coach,
making envious the stars,
fragrant the ambient air,
joyful the river-bank.
The foot that I adore
had scarce to emerald turned
the grass, the stream to crystal,
the sand to pearls, when sudden
—with copious discharge,
of rockets, balls and wheels—
the whole zone of fire
descended on the earth.
The sulphureous lights
still burning, those of four
and twenty cressets gan
the dimming of the stars.
First is heard the music
of the hautboys; then the viols
sound in the second tent;
from the third the flutes
with suavity are borne;
and in the fourth four voices
with harps and lutes resound.
The meantime have been served
full thirty banquet dishes,
first course and desserts,
all but as many, beside.
Fruits and wines in bowls
and goblets fashioned from
the crystal winter gives
and artifice preserves
are so deep frosted over
that Manzanares doubts
when through the Soto he goes—
he wends in the sierra.
Nor wants the sense of smell
when that of taste respites;

for with sweet-smelling spirits
of cassolettes and phials
and distilled essences
of perfumes, herbs and flowers,
the Soto of Madrid
was as the Sheban realm.
Thrust in a man of diamonds
dainty shafts of gold,
in which my lady might view
her rigour and my resolve,
reft their pre-eminence
from willow, reed and osier;
for when teeth are of pearl,
then haulms must be of gold.
And now, together mingled,
the four quires undertake
with separate accord
so to suspend the spheres
that envious Apollo
precipitates his course,
so the beginning day
may terminate the feast.

(*The Suspicious Truth*—Act I)

Miguel de Guevara (1585?–1646?)

SONNETS

1

"I am not moved to love thee, my Lord God"...

I am not moved to love thee, my Lord God,
By the heaven thou hast promised me;

I am not moved by the sore dreaded hell
to forbear me from offending thee.

I am moved by thee, Lord; I am moved
at seeing thee nailed upon the cross and mocked;
I am moved by thy body all over wounds;
I am moved by thy dishonor and thy death.

I am moved, last, by thy love, in such a wise
that though there were no heaven I still should love thee,
and though there were no hell I still should fear thee.

I need no gift of thee to make me love thee;
for though my present hope were all despair,
as now I love thee I should love thee still.

2

"Raise me up, Lord"...

Raise me up, Lord, who am fallen down,
void of love and fear and faith and awe;
I long to rise and in my place abide;
mine is the longing, mine the impediment.

I am, who am one only, cleft in twain;
I live and die, make merry and lament;
what I can do cannot by me be done;
I flee from evil and tarry in its toils.

I am so hardened in my obduracy
that spite the dread of losing me and thee
I never turn me from my wicked ways.

Between thy might and mercy I am torn;
in others every day I see amend,
in me I see fresh longing to offend thee.

3

"To crucify the Son"...

To Crucify the Son and pierce his breast,
to sacrify him that I might not die,
it is very sure proof, Lord, of love,
to show thyself so full of love for me.

So that—I God, thou mortal man—I should
give thee the godly being then were mine,
and in this my mortality lay me down
that of so good a God I might have joy.

And yet thy love received no recompense
when thou didst raise me up to excellency
of godhood, and to manhood God didst humble.

I owe and rightfully shall ever owe
the debt that by the Son upon the cross
was paid for me that thou mightst be requited.

4

"Time and account"

Time requires me to give account;
The account, if I would give it, requires time:

For he, without account, who lost such time,
How shall he, without time, give such account?

Time cares not to take time into account,
for the account was not made up in time;
for time would only take account of time
if in the account of time time found account.

What account shall suffice for so much time?
What time suffice for so great an account?
Life careless of account is shorn of time.

I live, I have no time, give no account,
knowing that I must give account of time
and that the time must come to give account.

Matías de Bocanegra (1612–1668)

Song on Beholding an Enlightenment

On an eve that May
chose to assay its powers,
portraying on the earth
the finery of heaven,
without fear nor doubt
it might, in such ostent,
rich, arrogant, presumptuous and proud,
be vanquished;
and as the westering sun
with incandescent light
fell whirling o'er the verge
—Phaeton headlong from
his ardent chariot hurled—
to burial in rosy sepulchre,

a mead appears,
spangled with flowers
in such luxuriance that it defies
and dares to vie with them as many stars
as shine upon the globe.

Sentinel stands
above this fair champaign
a Mountain, emerald
from peak to spacious lap;
Argus-like with white lilies
it is besprent and bright;
towering colossus,
rude Atlas of the skies,
lofty Polypheme
bruising with his brow the clouds,
and on whose pinnacle
a living fountain springs.
And finding no repose
in the close durance of its quiet bed,
the limpid Fount
channels its sands
and cunning vents
in threads of crystal, silver veins,
until impetuous
—its prison rent—
from the high peak it falls,
a snowy Icarus,
to gush in glassy coils
all down the Mountain's breast.
It comes to the fair lap
and frolicks joyfully
with gillyflowers and myrtles,
dewing with pearls their rubies;
and the mead, so imbued
with snow of running crystal,
puts forth fresh wreaths of flowers,

diversifies its hues,
in floral tribute making good as much
as from the stream it drank.

Thus richly clad the Mead,
when sorrowful
—stricken with fears,
his heart immersed in care—
upon the belvedere a Monk appeared
who could no longer
suffer his own self,
as by increasing pangs he is assailed;
with brimming eyes
and fitful pulse
and halting breath
and with a profane tumult in his thoughts.
To hill and dale,
seeing them thus adorned, he bends his gaze,
so haply they might still
the inner turmoil of his discourses.
Suspended all his sense
in a profound amaze,
on what he sees he lives;
for there he nought discerns
save only hill and field
that gently lull his grief
—as tumult slackens
and the close rig of pain
when falls the wind
that lashed the heart to storm—
till by a tuneful Goldfinch,
augur of calm to come,
he is aroused
from this dead life.

He lighted on a spray
of willow—verdant reef—

and in high counterpoint,
taking for theme his loves
and loving jealousies,
suspended heaven with his harmony.
Still be the strains
with which the Thracian charmed the savage beasts,
and hushed the tones
with which Amphion's lyre
gave movement to the stones,
and ended the grave harmony
in whose toils Arion took
the foaming dolphins:
for the Goldfinch had stayed
Phaeton in his career
were he not hindered, cracking his fiery whip,
from lending ear thereto.
The flowers at his coming joined
their plaudits, at his voice fell still,
and some to see him stood on their tiptoes.
The noisy brook
incontinent made halt,
its current left behind
—albeit quickened crystal, living ice—
and to its rapid steps
the sound of such sweet strains made obstacle.

The tuneful Goldfinch
checked his song and, the while,
free, joyous, sumptuous,
combed with his beak his wings;
like foam he ruffles
his gaudy plume
whose sheen the sun
oft envious shone upon.
Again he pipes
his boasted song
and the whole hemisphere

hangs on his melody,
and more ravished still
the sorry wretch
whose grievous adverse lot
turns all this suavity
to poisoned cup of bitterness.
And so, his slighted
heart dissolved
in fervent tears
welling from his eyes,
looking on the Goldfinch
—in contemplation of his blessed freedom—
he bespeaks him thus:

"Happy birdling
who dost sweetly sing
perched on these verdant shoots;
I grieve, thou jestest,
I complain while thou exultest;
the cause wherefor thou jestest and I grieve
is that thou art most alien from my grief,
and I hold manacled
the freedom, Goldfinch, that thou dost enjoy.
Ah, sweet freedom,
wasted in the flower of my years!
In bondage, gentle Goldfinch,
thou wouldest be less garrulous, I vow,
for thy dire pains
would tie thy tongue;
and prisoner moan
thy perished freedom, destitute of song.
Begone, confusion;
let now the spirit's perturbation cease;
in dread of what do I tremble
if to the world I also may take flight?

"If in crystal cradle

the Stream is born, and harks after its torrents,
finding its destined way
in perilous places,
in spite of crags and steeps,
and sundered seeking freedom;
if the Rose, in boastful beauty,
breaks the green bud's spiny clasp
to come abroad, fairest of all,
albeit the untimely birth
doom her to die to-morrow;
if the Fish, in windless depths
of Neptune's surging main,
joyous, despite the storm
that scours his domain,
comes safe from shore to shore
and—scaly vessel—cleaves the seas:
who do I hold
captive my freedom, I
whose empire is so free there is no might
may limit or pervert it?
In what law, Heaven, is it writ
that Stream, Rose, Fish and Bird,
born in servitude, shall enjoy
the liberty that never was their portion,
and I (absurdity!)
freeborn, not freely will?"

Thus he spoke,
and already made resolve
—blind and in despair--
to renounce his holy state,
when he beheld,
soaring, beating the air,
a Hawk appear
—Pirate whose sustenance
is plunder, feathered bolt,
wandering meteor, vertiginous comet.

Well armed with talons,
his beak a furbished sword,
he speeds his course,
spreading his body's sails.
Plumy craft, he towers
even to the clouds, to feign himself a cloud,
and thence—eyeing
the Goldfinch singing,
happy and careless,
heedless of peril,
the Hawk, poising,
stoops boltlike from the clouds
with such muffled thunder
that it is heard by none
but by the Bird who, terrorstruck,
beheld himself between the talons mangled
so unawares
that he together ended
his life and song,
breathing his latest accent from the wound,
leaving by his baneful death the flowers
beset with fears
and weeping piteously
such innocence so injured and aggrieved.

Then, full of horror,
and fresh affright,
the Monk, confused,
penitent, sorrowing,
learning from this strange hap
the cause of all his woe,
and bathed in tears
wrung from him by the violence of his grief,
desists from his intent
—his reason lit by God—
and makes him ready
with inward exhortation in this sort:

"See, soul, the liberty
that blind thou covetest,
for it is not fitting thou shouldst err
by ignorance in such a weighty matter.

"In a dead Goldfinch mark
thine own enlightenment,
and if its life deceived,
so may its death instruct thee.

"If in a cage the birdling
had been a prisoner,
on him, though seen, the Hawk
had never dared to seize.

"For living free he dies!
Oh cogent argument,
if bound the Bird is safe,
'tis freedom that destroys him!

"And were it not to stray
in grassy freedom, the Stream
would never know the steeps
towards which its waters flow.

"And were it not to range
the sea's immensities,
nor would the reckless Fish
lose freedom in the nets.

"And though the garden Rose
freed from its thorns expand,
full well it dreads the brute
and the audacious hand.

"And the Bird, though winged, beholds
himself to as many perils

a prey as the crafty Corsairs
that press him and assail.

"If Stream, Fish, Bird and Rose
for sake of freedom die,
by Fish, Bird, Stream and Rose,
'tis well thou shouldst be warned.

"For if I captive live,
a willing prisoner I;
and scorn, if free I die,
such heedless liberty."

Luis de Sandoval y Zapata

(MIDDLE OF SEVENTEENTH CENTURY)

SONNETS

1

*To the Admirable Transubstantiation
of the Roses into the marvellous image
of Our Lady of Guadalupe . . . the
Roses vanquish the Phoenix*

The Luminary of the Birds expires,
of the wind that winged eternity,
and midst the vapors of the monument
burns a sweet-smelling victim of the pyre.

And now in mighty metamorphosis
behold a shroud, with every flower more bright;
in the Cerecloth, reasonable essence,
the vegetable amber dwells and breathes.

The colours of Our Lady they portray;
and from these shades the day in envy flies
when the sun upon them shines his light.

You die more fortunate than the Phoenix, Flowers;
for he, feathered to rise, in ashes dies;
but you, Our Blessed Lady to become.

2

To Primal Matter

Within how many metamorphoses,
matter informed with life, hast thou had being?
Sweet-smelling snow of jessamine thou wast,
and in the pallid ashes didst endure.

Such horror by thee to thyself laid bare,
king of flowers, the purple thou didst don.
In such throng of dead forms thou didst not die,
thy deathbound being by thee immortalized.

For thou dost never wake to reason's light,
nor ever die before the invisible
murderous onset of the winged hours.

What, with so many deaths art thou not wise?
What art thou, incorruptible nature, thou
who hast been widowed thus of so much life?

3

To a Dead Actress

Here lies the purple sleeping and here lie
elegance and grace and loveliness,

and here that clarion of dulcitude
whose voice was lent to life's harmonious numbers.

Trumpet of love, no more thy clamant strain
with sonorous softness summons to the fray;
now in the tenebrous obscurity
with thine lies stricken many a tuneful soul.

Poesy thanks to thee was manifest
and with a fairer, surer life endued;
and—loving, cold, disdainful—thou didst feign

so well that even Death was unresolved
if thou didst simulate him as one dead
or didst submit to him as one alive.

4

White Lily

White Lily, thou who wast, unfurling wide
thy flaming spirit, brightness of the mead,
its green at dawn, its brightness in the sun,
its aery-throated snowy nightingale.

Tarnished crystal, yea, and withered gold,
the radiant light dissolved in dust of snow;
that it may seek the wandering monument,
now winged is the beauty of thy being.

Oh in exiguous silver candid flood!
In the bud of thy blooming thou didst find
an enemy scornful of thy loveliness;

and with the radiance of that ruby venom,
and with the gold, even when it was alive,
thou nowise didst redeem the debt of death.

5

Beauty on a Western Balcony

On the Occident she shed her light
who kindled in the Orient of beauty;
him to detain who hastened to his doom
the heaven of the West sought out the Sun.

I, in the Occident guitaring light,
in a love-distracted dying burned;
(the consummation of my little day
was Moon, because my life was up betimes).

Thou gainest from the Occident on the Sun;
fatal wounds he fugitive inflicts,
thou motionless inflictest wounds of healing.

In the Orient still he fans his pyres;
and thou, from out the West, a livelier Sun,
still fannest lives to life-consuming love.

6

Grievous Peril of a Gallant in Moth Metaphor

Animated glass that drawest nigh
unto the light, with thy life-freezing dark,

and from the fluttering circumference
pantest toward the sudden point of death.

In tiny sea of brightness gulfs of gloom
behold, thou ship that spreadest living sail;
the more funereal night of thy dismay
takes fire from the light thou comest to.

Let not thy coward spirit from the light
in which thou burnest turn aside its wings;
in the fire of thy seeking be consumed.

Joyfully amid its flames flagrate:
for ceasing to be that which thou hast lived
thou turnest into that which thou hast loved.

Carlos de Sigüenza y Góngora (1645–1700)

From the "Eastern Evangelic Planet"

To the Great Apostle of the Indies,
Saint Francis Xavier.

Invocation and Proposition

Thou, burning Topaz,
flaming spirit of the shining day,
whose inexhaustible diurnal monarchy
is by the courtiers idolized that haunt
that deathless Sapphire's palace,
now swifter wheel and bend
upon this feeble breast
the seas of splendour of thy placid fires.

Thou, Harmony of Heaven,
thou never sleeping, ever vigilant,
that from the lectern of Olympic diamond
intonest sweetly metered melody,
discharging to the skies
thy debt of stintless vigil,
now in harmonious cadency outpour
consonance of light and starry quires.

. . . Greatness of Xavier
—heroic enterprise—shall be my theme.
Enough, lascivious Grandson of the Foam,
of thy barbs' quivering coals;
for sweetly won
by a more sacred Love,
my rustic plectrum, moved by Helicon,
in brief conceit a wealth of feeling frames.

In ecstasy of love
the senses ravished, sweetly now they cleave
Eurus' transparent breast,
by gentle urges driven.
Hasten, Love, thy flight,
Beauteous Star of Heaven,
that borne on thy falling wings I may
come to the mighty halls of nascent light!

There where is dawning,
and on thrones of gold the glittering Diamond
scintillating dries with thirsty lip
the aromatic tears
shed by the wavering Dawn
on Flora's empire,
and where the Carnation, chill of sap,
nor wholly red abides, nor wholly dew.

There, where fragrant
floods of oriental gums condense

the air, and Arab spices
flying seek the castle of the Sun;
there, where canorous
the deathless Phoenix dwells
—heroic symbol, cast in coloured sphere,
of the great lastingness that shall be ours.

Juana de Asbaje (1651–1695)

1

Verses Expressing the Feelings of a Lover

My love, my lord,
hearken to my weary plaints awhile
as on the wind I cast them,
that it may wing them to thine ears,
so be it scatter not,
even as my hopes, the grievous voice.

With thine eyes hear me,
thou whose ears are so removed
from my pen murmuring
the groaning woes of absence;
and since my rude voice cannot come to thee,
deafly hear me, who mutely mourn.

If the fields are pleasant to thee,
joy in their happy verdancy,
untroubled by these faint
vexatious tears;
for there, attentive, thou wilt see
ensample of my woes and weal.

If thou seest the prattling stream,
lover of the meadow flowers,
impart with amorous flattery
to all it looks on its desire,
there flow my tears that thou mayst know
its laughter at my sorrow's cost.

If thou seest the turtle-dove
plaintive on a green bough mourning
its withered hope,
let bough and dove remind thee of my grief,
for they set forth, in greenness and lament,
my hope and pain.

If thou seest the fragile flower,
the crag that proudly scorns
the spurning tread of time,
both image me, albeit differently,
that my contentment, this my obduracy.

If thou seest the wounded stag
that hastens down the mountain-side,
seeking, stricken, in icy stream
ease for its hurt,
and thirsting plunges in the crystal waters,
not in ease, in pain it mirrors me.

If from the savage hounds
the timorous hare in terror flies
and leaves no trace, that it may live,
of its light feet,
so my hope, in doubting and misgiving,
is close pursued by cruel jealousies.

If thou seest the bright sky,
even such is my soul's purity;
and if the day, niggard of light,

wraps its radiancy in gloom,
its darkness and inclemency
image my life since thou art gone.

Thus, sweet Fabio,
thou mayst with tranquil mind
have tidings of my woes,
perusing nature's face,
and as to every thing I fit my grief,
know my pain and still thy pleasure take.

But when alas! my glory, shall I have
my meed of joyance in thy tranquil light?
When will it be, the day
when thou shall put sweet end to so much pain?
When, dear enchantment, shall I see thine eyes
and tears desist from mine?

When will thy sounding voice
strike softly on mine ear,
and the soul that adores thee,
flooded with spate of joy,
to welcome thee with loving haste
shine forth dissolved in gladness?

When will thy fair light bathe
my sense in splendour?
And I, for happiness,
and soon to hold the guerdon of my tears,
count my vain sighs for nought?
—For such is joy and such the price of pain.

When shall I see the pleasant aspect
of thy gentle joyous face
and that unspeakable boon
no human pen can tell?

—For how should that which overflows the whole
of sense within the finite be contained?

Come then, beloved treasure,
for already my weary life is dying
of this sore absence;
come then, for while thou tarriest thy coming,
my hope, although its greenness cost me dear,
is watered by mine eyes.

2

Describes Rationally the Irrational Effects of Love

This torment of love
that is in my heart,
I know I feel it
and know not why.

I feel the keen pangs
of a frenzy desired
whose beginning is longing
and end melancholy.

And when I my sorrow
more softly bewail,
I know I am sad
and know not why.

I feel for the juncture
I crave a fierce panting,
and when I come nigh it
withhold mine own hand.

For if haply it offers
after much weary vigil,

mistrust spoils its savour
and terror dispels it.

. . . .

Now patient, now fretful,
by conflicting griefs torn,
who for him much shall suffer,
and with him suffer nought.

. . . .

On scant foundations
my sad cares raise
with delusive conceits
a mountain of feeling.

And when that proud mass
falls asunder I find
that the arrogant fabric
was poised on a pin.

Beguiled perhaps by grief
I presume without reason
no fulfilment can ever
my passion assuage.

. . . .

And though nigh disabused,
still the same grief assails me,
that I suffer so sore
for so little a cause.

Perhaps the wounded soul sweeping
to take its revenge
repents it and wreaks
other vengeance on me.

. . . .

In my blindness and folly
I, gladly deceived,
beseech disenchantment
and desire it not.

3

"Tarry, shadow of my scornful treasure" . . .

Tarry, shadow of my scornful treasure,
image of my dearest sortilege,
fair illusion for which I gladly die,
sweet unreality for which I painfully live.

To the compelling magnet of thy grace
since my breast as docile steel is drawn,
why dost thou with soft ways enamour me
if from me then in mockery thou must fly?

And yet thou mayst nowise in triumph boast
that over me thy tyranny has prevailed;
for though thou breakest, mocking, the narrow coil

that girdled thy fantastic form about,
what boots it to make mock of arms and breast
if thou art prisoner of my fantasy?

4

"Diuturnal infirmity of hope". . .

Diuturnal infirmity of hope,
thou that sustainest thus my fainting years,
and on the equal edge of weal and woe
holdest in equilibrium the scales

forever in suspense, forever loath
to tilt, thy wiles obeying that forbid
the coming ever to excess of measure
either of confidence or of despair.

Who rid thee of the name of homicide?
For thou art crueler still, if well we mark
that thou suspendest the deluded soul

between a wretched and a happy lot,
not to the end that life may be preserved,
but to inflict a more protracted death.

5

"This evening when I spake with thee, beloved" . . .

This evening when I spake with thee, beloved,
as in thy face and in thy mien I saw
that I could not persuade thee with my words,
the longing came for thee to see my heart,

and love, abettor of my purposes,
accomplished that which seemed impossible,
for issuing with the tears that sorrow shed
the heart dissolved in misery distilled.

Enough of cruelty, beloved, enough:
let my harsh jealousy torment thee not
nor vile suspicion violate thy virtue

with foolish shadows, vain appearances,
since now in aqueous humour thou hast seen
and held between thy hands my broken heart.

6

"This coloured counterfeit that thou beholdest" . . .

This coloured counterfeit that thou beholdest,
vainglorious with the excellencies of art,
is, in fallacious syllogisms of colour,
nought but a cunning dupery of sense;

this in which flattery has undertaken
to extenuate the hideousness of years,
and, vanquishing the outrages of time,
to triumph o'er oblivion and old age,

is an empty artifice of care,
is a fragile flower in the wind,
is a paltry sanctuary from fate,

is a foolish sorry labour lost,
is conquest doomed to perish and, well taken,
is corpse and dust, shadow and nothingness.

7

"Divine rose, that in a pleasant garden". . .

Divine rose, that in a pleasant garden,
persuasive with sweet-smelling subtlety,
in crimson mastery impartest beauty
and snowy disciplines of loveliness.

Intimation of the human frame,
epitome of unavailing grace,
in whose being nature did unite
the joyful cradle and the fearsome tomb.

How haughty in thy pomp, presumptuous
and proud, thou dost disdain the threat of death,
and then, dismayed and humbled, showest forth

thy perishable being's withered marks!
Thus with learned death and ignorant life
living thou dost deceive and dying teach.

8

"Crimson lute that comest in the dawn". . .

Crimson lute that comest in the dawn
with doleful ditty to thy cherished mate
and in the amber of the nutrient rose
stainest coral red thy golden beak.

Gentle goldfinch, birdling born to sorrow,
that scarce didst glimpse the lovely break of day
when, at the first note of thy melody,
thou wast by death received, by song abandoned.

In life there is no sure lot, verily;
with thine own voice thou callest on the hunter
that he fail not to strike thee with his shaft.

Oh dreaded destiny and yet pursued!
Oh passing belief that thine own life should be,
rather than silent, privy to thy death!

9

"Green enravishment of human life". . .

Green enravishment of human life,
smiling frenzy of demented hope,
inextricable dream of them that wake
and, as a dream, of riches destitute.

Spirit of the world, robust old age,
imagination of decrepit vigour,
longing for the happy ones' to-day
and for the unhappy ones' to-morrow.

Let those who, with green glasses spectacled,
see all things sicklied o'er with their desire,
questing for thy light pursue thy shadow:

but I, more mindful of my destiny,
imprison my two eyes in my two hands
and see no other thing than it I touch.

10

"Amorous of Laura's loveliness". . .

Amorous of Laura's loveliness
the heavens rapt her to their high abode,
it ill befitting her pure light to shed
its radiancy on these unhappy vales,

or to the end that mortal men, deceived
by the perfection of her bodily frame,
should not imagine, in their wonderment
at so much beauty, theirs a blessed lot.

Born where the red veil of the orient
falls from the dawning of the roseate face,
she died where the deep sea, with avid zest,

gives sepulchre to its effulgency;
it being ordained her godlike flight should cast,
even as the Sun, a girdle round the world.

11

Christmas Hymn

This shepherdess
serene of gaze,
charm of the grove,
envy of the sky,

she whose eye smote,
whose lock ensnared,
the Shepherd of
the supernal fire.

To whom her lover
was myrrh a space
in the bower
of her white breasts.

She who in rich
apparel adorns

the cedarn house,
the flowery bed.

She who made boast
her dusky hue
was kindled by
the Phoebean rays.

For whom her Spouse
in ardent vigil
sped his way
o'er hill and dale.

She soft of speech
from whose fair lips
nectar, milk
and honey flow.

She who would know
with anxious love
where her Spouse
grazes his lambs.

To whom her lover,
generous and fond,
from Libanus sweetly
suppliant calls.

To enjoy the arms
of her loving lord,
she leaves the low vale
for the lofty mount.

The sacred shepherds
of eternal Olympus
hail her coming
with dulcet song.

But those of the vale,
as they watch her fly,
utter sudden
troubled murmurs.

12

First Dream

But Venus first
with her fair gentle morning-star
shone through the dayspring,
and old Tithonus' beauteous spouse
—Amazon in radiance clad—
armed against the night,
fair though martial
and though plaintive brave,
showed her lovely brow
crowned with morning glimmers,
tender yet intrepid harbinger
of the fierce luminary
that came, mustering his van
of tiro gleams
and his rearward
of stouter veteran lights
against her, usurping tyrant
of day's empire, who,
girt with gloom's black bays
sways with dread nocturnal sceptre
the shades,
herself by them appalled.
But the fair forerunner,
herald of the bright sun,
scarce flew her banner in the orient sky,

calling all the sweet if warlike
clarions of the birds to arms,
their featly artless
sonorous bugles,
when the doomed tyrant, trembling,
distraught with dread misgiving,
striving the while
to launch her vaunted might, opposing
the shield of her funereal cloak
in vain to the unerring
shafts of light
with the rash unavailing
valiance of despair,
sensible of her faintness to withstand,
prone already to commit to flight,
more than to might, the means of her salvation,
wound her raucous horn,
summoning her black battalions
to orderly retreat.
Forthwith she was assailed
with nearer plenitude of rays
that streaked the highest pitch
of the world's lofty towers.
The sun in truth, its circuit closed, drew near,
limning with gold on sapphire blue a thousand
times a thousand points and gleaming scarves,
and from its luminous circumference
innumerable rays of pure light streamed,
scoring the sky's cerulean plain,
and serried fell on her who was but now
the baneful tyrant of their empire.
She, flying in headlong rout,
mid her own horrors stumbling,
trampling on her shade,
strove, with her now blindly fleeing host
of shadows harried by the overtaking light,
to gain the western verge which loomed at last

before her impetuous course.
Then, by her very downfall vivified,
plunging in ever more precipitant ruin,
with renewed rebellion she resolves,
in that part of the globe
forsaken by the day,
to wear the crown,
what time upon our hemisphere the sun
the radiance of his fair golden tresses shed,
with equable diffusion of just light
apportioning to visible things their colours
and still restoring
to outward sense its full efficacy,
committing to surer light
the world illuminated and myself awake.

(fragment from the *First Dream*)

José Manuel Martínez de Navarrete (1768–1809)

Morning

The candid morn already lifts on high
her peaceful brow; already the eastern sky
is flooded with resplendency of rays
that lights up the whole countenance of heaven.

As if dismayed the shadows fly away
to the opposing verge. I seem to feel
our globe, that even now was as though held
suspended in the heavy hand of night,
turn on its massy axles. In an instant
the world entire is astream with joy.

Pleasurable spectacle! What eyes,
what breast can contemplate the blessed day

and not be moved by its miraculous light?
Already in the air a freshness stirs,
restoring with its animating breath
all the beings that beautify the earth.
The amber of the flowers already wafts
its sweetness to the atmosphere; and all
the plants in the green valley are revived
by the pervasive sap that permeates
the secret channels of their dainty veins.
The whole of fertile nature, joyously,
rises in gladness, lovely to behold,
and seems awaked by an invisible hand
that it may enter on its offices.
The voices of the innocent singing birds
echo and echo again among the hills;
a whisper rustles through the leafy groves
and, frolicking, the murmurous rivulet
gurgles gleefully o'er its pebbly bed.

Among the fields what salutary hours
are those that come with the first morning light,
bringing fresh vigour to the languid limbs,
those hours that in their downy beds the pale
and ailing citizens let slip away!
All things quicken in the soul a zest
that unto grand and lofty meditation
elevates it with mysterious urge.
All things are imprinted with the mark
of their eternal Maker. Every being,
each one according to his fashion, seems
to praise the bountiful creating hand.

In lively motion everything is set:
each artless one of them that sojourn here
begins his labours with the break of day.
Following her flock of snowy sheep
the gentle shepherdess makes joyful play,

tressing a garland that she beautifies
with various flowers for her candid brow.
The neatherd manages his crowding kine
that scatter on the pretty common land:
the robust ploughman gets him ready for
the cultivation of the fertile soil.

I go to the cornfield that Providence
assigns to me with his invisible hand:
I shall endure the ardent sun; yet glad
with the abundant seasonable grain
given me by the furrows that I tend,
assuaged the heat of evening, I shall turn
my steps towards my enviable cot,
abode of peace and haven of delights,
where my beloved spouse, with open arms,
already waits for me. My little ones,
greeting me with many a joyous frolick,
will hang about my neck: and verily
mine then will be the semblance of the tree
bowed down beneath the sweetest clusters of all.

And shall I then give up my cottage home,
confined and lowly though it be, to dwell
in sumptuous palace, where a wealthy lord,
resplendent as the sun within its sphere,
treads deep in carpets overlaid with gold?
Never. Nor shall I change this instrument,
however rustic and uncouth it be,
this benefactor that provides me with
my needs in all my life's emergencies,
for the refulgent sceptre that a monarch
wields in his all-powerful right hand.

There is not room within my breast to hold
my joy, nor do I cease to praise at morn
the universal sire of all creation,
whom in that dawning light I contemplate,

nor doing so desist from seeing him
in all his other mighty works besides,
how vast in number, kind and wondrousness!
But none so lovely as the lovely dawn
that seems to quicken all the others, shedding
the light upon them of her countenance.

Oh smile of heaven's face and cheerfulness
of these felicitous pastures! I salute thee,
harbinger of the resplendent sun.
The fresh shades and the verdant champaign land,
the limpid fountains and the balmy zephyrs,
the tender flowers and melodious birds,
salute thee also in their various ways.

Now the whole of nature seems to raise
its lovely face from out the sepulchre.
All its creatures quicken to new life
in the pleasant sweetness of thy presence;
to their deep lairs the savage beasts make haste,
the goats begin to frisk, the sheep to bleat,
the kine to call out to their little calves,
the bulls to bellow and echo to respond,
reverberated by the iterant hills.
The shepherds and the shepherdesses sing
sweet-sounding hymns to the eternal Maker,
who inundates thy glorious countenance
with such glad light to look upon the morn.

José Joaquín Pesado (1801–1861)

The Huntress

In hot career or ranging far and wide,
gentle huntress, you speed your onward way,

abandoning upon the gusty air
the tossing feather of your gallant hat.

Over brake and barrier, without pause,
panting, your impetuous courser bounds,
and across the arid torrents storms,
beating the boulders with his thudding hooves.

And before you, chaser of the wild,
the peopled mountain yields, and in its glass
the tarn exhibits you victorious.

The mob breaks forth in turbulent applause,
and to the sudden clamour of your name
the mighty forest, sonorous, made reply.

Ignacio Rodríguez Galván (1816–1842)

Extract from the Prophecy of Cuauhtémoc

Space is azure and the mountains bathe
in vivid azure and in azure shade.
The breath of blithesome youth is everywhere,
and the singing birds toss to and fro
upon the gentle breezes' restlessness.
All things incite to joy; and yet my soul
is muffled in a cloak of death; and drop
by drop my wounded heart bleeds slow away.
My mind is a black bottomless abyss,
and in it thought goes blindly wandering
like a lost dove in an unfathomed cave.

Was it reality or dream? . . . Vain question. . . .
A dream assuredly, for a deep dream

is the voracious passion that consumes me;
it was a dream, no more, the joy that touched
my cheek with faint caress; a dream the accents
of that voice that lulled my grief to sleep;
a dream that smile, a dream that blandishment
and that soft gaze . . . I suddenly awoke;
and the fair Eden vanished from my sight
as the wave that rides in from the sea
and scatters; there is nothing left to me
except the cruel memory that wrings
my soul and without ceasing gnaws my heart.

.   .   .   .

Make haste, dreams, make haste! And deck my brow
with deadly nightshade: I desire to dream.
From their graves resuscitate the dead,
that I may see them, touch them, shuddering . . .
I have fed my life with what I felt,
with the horror I felt and with the sorrow.
Dream, in thy safe keeping let me come
to this world's end. . . .

Ignacio Ramírez (1818–1879)

For the Dead Gregorians . . .

What! would you have the fatal sister lend
an ear to sorrow's pleas? Vain intercession!
Rabble of spectres, get you to your dens!

Separated brother was from brother!
To sit us down at table it is too late;
to get us gone with you it is too soon!

For you, unhappy ones, no longer burns

a single log upon the hearth; nor do
I see that any cup awaits your kisses.

A sigh goes after you, a sigh, no more!
Peace be with your going; and may fortune
not bar the way to your retreat to light.

I hate the sepulchre, changed to the cradle
of a vile insect or a venomous snake,
where the sun never rises, nor the moon.

May among your bones a rose take root,
reigned over by the painted butterfly,
and with its fragrance permeate the dew.

Hearken fearless to the impious thunder:
and smile in contemplation, near at hand,
of a stream swollen, overflowing with life.

To get us gone with you it is too soon!
Let her consent at least, the Furious One,
to wait until the cup slips from our hand.

Why, more swiftly still alas! than you,
why does she strip us of existence bare?
From one she steals his forehead's ornament,

another with her rude hand bends in twain:
some she envelops in a yellow veil:
and others in their entrails feel a claw

that rends, and in their veins an icy cold.
Alas! the spring will come again and find
sorrow in our gates, and lamentation.

And we shall watch the feasters from without.
Perhaps for one the hour has come to go!
The throng of spectres watches for his going.

The course that we are setting, do you know
for what port it is bound? The tomb. Our ship
already founders. Shivered, the mast falls.

Some lie drifting in the waters, dying.
Others commit them to the fragile raft;
and for him who climbed into the shrouds

hope's despairing light still gutters on,
while wind and wave concert their batteries
and the implacable sky lets loose its bolts.

The flames mount to the lowering of the pennons,
unknown to all save to the bird of rapine,
the sullen west and monsters of the deep.

What is our life but an ill-fashioned vase
whose worth is but the worth of the desire
shut up in it by nature and by chance?

When I see it spilt by age I know
that in the hand of the wise earth alone
it can receive new form and new employ.

Life is not life, but prison, in which want
and pain and lamentation pine in vain;
pleasure flown, who is afraid of death?

Mother nature, there are no more flowers
along the slow paths of my stumbling feet.
I was born without hope or fear;
fearless and hopeless I return to thee.

Vicente Riva Palacio (1832–1896)

To the Wind

When I was a child I lay in dread,
listening to you moaning at my door,
and fancying I heard the sorrowful
and grievous dirge of some unearthly being.

When I was a youth your tumult spoke
phrases with meaning that my mind divined;
and, blowing through the camp, in after years
your harsh voice kept on crying "Fatherland."

Now, in the dark nights, I hear you beating
against my incoercible prison-bars;
but my misfortunes have already told me

that you are wind, no more, when you complain,
wind when raging, wind when murmuring,
wind when you come and wind when you depart.

Ignacio Manuel Altamirano (1834–1893)

To the Atoyac

July sun burns down on the sandy beaches
lashed by the breakers of the angry sea,
and in their turbulence the arrogant waters
pit their harsh roar against the ardent rays.

You flow softly in the pleasant shade
shed for you by the branchy mangrove-tree:
and on the mossy carpet spangled o'er
with sweet spring flowers your sleeping pools repose.

You frolic in the grots your banks recess
among the vast wood's mahoes and cotton-trees,
and murmur tranquilly beneath the palms
slenderly mirrored in your crystal wave.

This heavenly Eden that here the coast secludes
is sheltered from the sun's candescent rays;
its light falls warm and gentle through the trees
and takes a green tinge from their spreading boughs.

Here all is hush of sweet unnumbered murmurs,
the whisper softly flowing of your waters,
the growing plant, the music of the birds,
the sighing breeze and rocking of the branches.

The flowers flaunt that from your canopy hang
in countless garlands to adorn your brow,
and the huge lotus, springing from your bed,
with its fresh clusters bends towards you too.

The papaw-tree stoops quivering to your lap,
the mango with its gold and carmine drupes.
And in the poplars the gay parrot flutters
with the harsh pecker and the tuneful linnet.

Sometimes your glassy sheen is struck to foam
on every side by your dark wantoning nymphs;
you fondle them with many a secret clasp
and languidly receive their loving kisses.

And when the sun is hidden by the palms
and in your wilding temple darkness gathers,

the birds salute you with their parting songs
borne by the last breath of the wind away.

Night falls warm; already the white moon
hangs shining in the midst of sapphire sky,
and in your wildwood all is rapt and stilled
and on your margins all begins to sleep.

Then in your sandy bed, bemused, beneath
the melancholy mantle of the palms,
scarcely illumined by the silver light
of the great star of night, you also sleep.

Thus soft you glide; and neither the faint stir
of boats and oars disturb your rest, nor yet
the sudden leaping of the fish that flies
in fear towards the rocks the fisher shuns;

nor the chirp of crickets from the creeks,
nor the snails' roundelay upon the air,
nor the curassow, whose plaintive cries
distract the cayman's sleep among the reeds.

What time the fireflies with gleaming dust
sprinkle the shady herbage of the canes
and the dark mallows of the springing cotton
that grows in the ditch, amid the stalky maize.

And the maiden in the cabin, rocking
on the light hammock languid to and fro,
sings the samba's saddening lullaby
and singing sighs and sighing ever sings.

But of a sudden from the shore a harp
sounds on the air with urgent clanging strings,
tumultuous prelude to the flower of songs,
the sweet malagueña that makes glad the heart.

Then from the villages hard upon the harp
the joyous throng begins to scour the woods,
and soon upon your margin all is joy
and dance and song and love and merriment.

So haste away the brief unheeded hours.
And from the torpor of your gentle dreams
you hearken to your dark enticing daughters
intoning to the moon their hymns of love.

The nestling birds are tremulous with joy;
the opening magnolias shed their nectar;
the zephyrs wake and seem to sigh; your waters
feel how they palpitate within their bed.

Alas! in these hours when burning sleeplessness
revives the memory of blessings gone,
who does not seek the absent love's soft breast
whereon to press his lips and lay his head?

The palms together twine; caressing light
evinces dismal darkness from your bed;
the flowers flood the breezes with their sweets. . . .
The soul alone feels its sad solitude!

Farewell, quiet stream; the doles of sorrow
do not grieve your green and smiling banks;
for they are for the lonely rocks alone,
lashed by the breakers of the angry sea.

The moon sleeps mirrored in your crystal waters
that overlap your shrubby banks and rock
the bluey sedges and green galingale
drooping now in drowsiness again.

You flow softly in the pleasant shade
shed for you by the branchy mangrove-tree;
and on the mossy carpet spangled o'er
with sweet spring flowers your sleeping pools repose.

Joaquín Arcadio Pagaza (1839–1918)

1

The Crag

On the mountain's blind and rugged ridge
and dizzy pinnacle its throne is set;
its crown is laurel and its canopy
the clouds and the cerulean firmament.

Its fearful grasp is sceptered haughtily
with a green boulder of enormous mass;
the hills are subject to its majesty,
the far-flung valley is its empire.

It pours upon its awesome countenance,
its lofty port and dreadful attitude,
dark in the burnished crystal of the mere;

and its most sweet and pleasant music is
the flashing thunder and the desolate
screaming of the savage towering eagle.

2

The Chest of Perote

Majestuous and sapphirine, it rears
its lonely bulk towards the high serene,
disdainful of the soft and verdant bed,
gazing on the Atlantic at its feet.

A royal diadem of spotless white
encircles glittering its frosty brow;
and over cheeks and throat the impetuous beard
scatters a tumultuous covering.

In the warm season it lies overspread
with a great sullen stooping cloud, until
the bleak face darkens with a great amaze;

panting, it huddles on its cloak of mist,
louder and louder growls its growing rage,
hurls stone and scree, shudders and fulminates.

Manuel M. Flores (1840–1885)

Eve

To Rosario de la Peña

It was the sixth dawn. Still the *Fiat Lux*
resounded in the deep
expanse of air;
it was the calm awakening of the world
within the cradle of time.
It was the dawn,
and the Creator, with his sovereign hand,
circled with gauze of topaz and of rose,
fit for the chaste brow of a bride, the chaste
brow of the morn.

The golden waves of the primeval light
rippled on the unsubstantial air,
and lifting modestly her veil the spring,
the gentle spring, resplendently adorned,

went forth among the virgin fields of earth,
freshening the flowers with her beating wings.

The blue mount, yielding up its granite peak
to the caresses of the clouds whose fleece
is scattered through the infinite of air,
unfolded over emerald fields the abundant
kirtle of its wild and quiet woods,
and a curtain of moving foliage,
cascading verdurous
into the gorges,
gave shade and freshness to the grottoes hung
with sweet red roses and white jessamine.

The tangled wood, presentient of the day,
peopled its bosky haunts with murmurous sound;
through the midst of trembling reeds and rushes,
frolicksome, the joyous water sped.
On the flowers the angel of the mist
scattered pearly moisture from his wings,
and Aurora floated on the air,
enveloped in her gauzy topaz robe.

It was the nuptial hour. The earth lay sleeping,
virginal, beneath the bashful veil,
and to surprise her with his amorous kisses
the royal sun inflamed the firmament.
It was the nuptial hour. All the waters
of the streams, the fountains and the seas,
preluding in ineffable harmony,
quired a measure from the Song of Songs.

The sacred incense of the fragrancy
effused abroad by all the flower-cups
floated on the zephyrs with it fraught,
that to the music of their wings rehearsed
a concert and of kisses and of sighs;

and as many birds of canorous strain
as soar in the diaphanous heights of air
poured forth their harmonies upon the wind
and unleashed the torrent of their songs.

It was the nuptial hour. Nature still
bedazzled by her issuing forth from chaos,
intoxicated with her youth and beauty,
sacred and virginal,
veiling her face in poetry and mystery,
offered, upon earth's thalamus of roses,
herself to man.

Man! . . . There in the deep
and innermost recesses of the wood,
where the shadow of the gentle palm
was mildest and the mossy carpet most soft
and the lemon-tree most rich and fragrant;
where the flowers crowded loveliest
and by the breeze and by the brook was borne
the most of perfume and the most of murmur;
where the warbling of the nightingales
was sweetest, and the mourning of the doves,
and the hesitating twilight spread
its fairest veils,
there man lay sleeping,
there in his dwelling-place, in Paradise.

The spotless world
was born in grandeur and serenity;
God looked upon creation
and saw that it was good.

Bathed in splendour, saturate with dawn,
in the hallowed quiet of that hour,
in the sleeping shadow of that palm,
in the lap of that beflowered sward,

Adam lay, his manly head at rest
on his strong arm,
and on the wanton breeze his gentle locks
dishevelled strayed; and yet his lofty brow
predestined to the crown, his noble face
august with beauty in the midst of sleep,
reflected an austere and sombre sorrow.
The morning zephyr gently eddying
caressed his brow, and his breast softly rose
and softly fell;
and yet there issued from his parted lips
a breath that was as though he breathed a sigh.
Did he suffer? . . . The Creator
alone in that retreat was with the sleeper.

He was the first of men, the moment was
the first of his existence, and already
the voice of suffering faltered on his lips.
The vast void palpitated all about,
yet he was solitary. Solitude
transformed the sovereign into an outcast . . .
Then it was the hand of the Creator
stretched forth and touched an instant Adam's side.

.   .   .   .

Suave, indistinct, sidereal, hovering,
like the light vapour rising from the foam,
like the white beam of the moon that goes
wandering through a rack of shadowy mist,
chaste emanation, most chaste and serene,
issuing from the lily's virgin chalice,
living pearl of the fair dawn of day,
light forerunner of the light to come
and gathered into the voluptuous form
of a new being quickening into life,
white and luminous a figure rose
by the side of Adam, sleeping Adam.

The first of womankind! Effulgent sky
that with thy light didst bathe this firstling morn,
hast thou beheld from that time forth to now,
among the vast throng of humanity's daughters,
one more entrancing, gracious, perfect than
that first of womankind?

The selfsame hand that garmented the earth
with blue horizons,
the fields with emerald,
with snow the mountain's summit and its slopes
with deepest green;
that same which from the waves of the dark sea
strikes plumes of shining foam
and crowns with rainbow and with mist the swift
and savage cataract;
that selfsame which imbues with magic colours
the flowers and the feathers of the birds;
that same which to such beauty paints the clouds
of crimson, gold and opal that compose
the distant prospects of the evening sky;
that same which in the crystal dome of air
suspends the frigid moon's opacous globe
and to the glorious zenith lifts on high
the diadem of the day-dispensing sun;
that same which, spreading the transparent veil
of the wide firmament, left on heaven's face,
as though forgotten by its fingers of light,
the radiant dust of stars;
that same from which perennially outpours
the stintless prodigies of mighty nature;
the hand of the Eternal God of beauty,
oh first of womankind . . . that same made thee!

The sweet pallor of the lily opening
with dawn
and the chaste radiance of the moon at full

bestowed on the enchantment of her face
their purity and light. The taintless lips
than which the reddest rose is not more red,
that gaze in whose wide-open lustrous eyes
the spirit shines,
and over the white neck,
apparelling voluptuously her spells,
the cascade of her luxuriant tresses
pouring down in waves of flowing curls.

Her chaste nakedness shone forth, her lips
smiled and her breath
perfumed the air;
and there was kindled by her gazing eyes
an unutterable light that mingled
with the uncertain twilight of the dawn. . . .
Eve was the flowering soul of Paradise.

And all about her then there was a stir
of rich and joyous life;
all nature trembling, even as a lover
the trembling virgin, clasped her tenderly.
For her the breezes and the foliage sang
the song of their melodious murmuring,
sang it to the rhythm of living waters
rolling their sonorous and crystal torrents.

Gentle zephyrs, wafting to and fro,
saturated with their scents her tresses,
fleeting murmurs sighed upon the air,
and the warbling of the nightingales
was sweeter, and the mourning of the doves;
and all the while the roses, rapturous,
moist already with the celestial dew,
bathed with fragrant essences her feet
and then drooped down towards her with their kisses.

The sun was almost risen; dawn was breaking,
and in the peaceful shadow of the palm
quietly Adam slept. The passing breeze
brushed with caressing wing the majestic brow
and a smile trembled on the parted lips.
Eve looked on him,
her hand upon her troubled heart, her eyes,
her sovereign eyes already languishing,
moist and fraught with love;
and little by little, tremulous, distraught,
feeling within her overpowered breast
the fervid palpitating of her heart,
and feeling that her being was possessed
by some ineffable resistless power
that down towards the gentle sleeper's lips
impelled her own,
she stooped to him. . . .
                                        And suddenly
a quivering kiss was heard, and Paradise
trembled with love. . . .

And the sun at that instant raised his brow!

José Peón y Contreras (1843–1907)

Echoes

When in the ardent spells
of your pale beauty I,
like many a one before,
sought your smile and eyes,
for whom, then, was your smile,
terrifying statue, say?
For whom the steadfast look
of your unseeing eyes?

Justo Sierra (1848–1912)

Bucolic Funeral

Incipe Maenalios mecum mea tibia verens
Virgil Ecl. VIII

1

In the pallid soughing of the dawn
the moon extinguishes her crystal sphere,
and from the sea the fresh and sounding breeze
wanders among the pines along the shore.

Here in a fatal hour Mirtilo died
of love; his sheep are crying and the spring
is crying and the flowers, with rustic incense,
whose fumes intoxicate, are paying tribute.

Yonder stands the pyre; and round about
the shepherds crowned with cypress and verbena
begin to tread a grave and grievous measure;

the wood with murmurous suavity complains,
and there, among Mirtilo's flowers, lies
the sweet oat-grass as well, that scents of honey.

2

But in the east the morning scarcely smiles
when to the place the flocking shepherds throng;
they join their voices in the dolesome chant,
and the sweet-smelling violets unfold.

Now the measures turn in living garlands;
now they quicken to an ardent rhythm

reiterated in the nearby stream
by laughing dryads and lascivious fauns.

Phoebus darts his diamond javelin;
the dance impetuous wheels; the shepherds loose
from their sore-burdened breasts a frenzied cry

of love, that makes the fiery welkin ring.
At that instant innocent Mirtilo
lacked but a kiss to bring him back to life.

3

With the tumult of the open lips'
convulsive sobs the sudden clamour mingles,
and down into the red mouths is received
the burning weeping of the flowing eyes.

Homage to Mirtilo! How could his shades
remain indifferent to such a quire?
Wafted by love and in a bark of gold
far from his native songs his spirit flies.

The pure milk froths in newly fashioned bowls,
and from their bosomed plenitude they pour
its glossy whiteness, torrent after torrent.

On the aromatic funeral pile
the fire laps at last the gloomy pyre,
and in the sapphire calm the sun ascends.

4

The fire waxes, sets its angry teeth
into the boughs, whose spices cloy the wind;
and the dance dies, when the last flame breathes
on the last thistle its expiring breath.

Black and red the earthen urn in which
the shepherds instantly receive the ashes,
and they commit to a rude monument
with pious care the piteous remains.

Mirtilo is asleep; the shadowy grove
that pours on thy deserted sepulchre
its tranquil and ineffable poetry

will not forget thy grievous destiny,
nor the transient elegy of thy love,
nor with death thy nuptials everlasting.

Manuel Acuña (1849–1873)

Before a Corpse

Well! there you lie already ... on the board
where the far horizon of our knowledge
dilates and darkens to a vaster verge.

Where implacable experience
unanswerably states the higher laws
to which existence is subservient.

Where that glorious luminary shines
whose light extinguishes the difference
that separates the master from the slave.

Where the voice of fable is heard no more
and reality speaks out aloud
and superstition vanishes away.

Where crisis presses on to where it may
decipher the solution of the problem
whose mere enouncement fills us with dismay,

that which arises from a premised reason
and hangs upon your lips to be unsealed
in the tremendous voice of final truth.

There you lie . . . beyond the ignoble strife
in which it was vouchsafed to you at last
to break the bonds that held you fast to pain.

There is no more light within your eyes,
lifeless and inert your tenement rests,
its end forsaken and its means destroyed.

Vanitas! they seeing you will say
whose creed is that the empire of life
ends at the point where that of death begins.

And deeming that your mission is fulfilled,
they will come to you and with their eyes
wish you for eternity farewell.

But it is false! . . . your mission is not fulfilled,
for out of nothingness we are not born,
and into nothingness we do not die.

Existence is a circle, and we err
when we assign to it for measurement
the limits of the cradle and the grave.

The mother is the mould, and nothing more,
that gives us form, the transitory form
with which we make our thankless way through life.

Yet neither was that form the first assumed
by our existence, neither will it be,
to-morrow, when it perishes, the last.

Yet a little and you, your last breath sped,
will be restored to earth and to its womb
which is the source of universal life.

And there your dust, in seeming so remote
from life, will quicken once again beneath
the fecundating might of rain and summer.

And with the springing up from root to grain,
a witness to the plant you will arise
to the high realm of sovereign alchemy;

or it may be, converted into corn,
returned to the sad hearth where the sad spouse,
wanting for bread, is with you in her dreams.

What time the larva from your cloven grave's
uncovered depths ascends, its being changed
into the being of a butterfly,

and faltering in its first uncertain flight,
comes to the desolate pillow of your love,
bearer of your kisses from the dead.

And in the midst of all this inner change
your skull, instinct with an impetuous life,
instead of thoughts will bring forth flowers, flowers

within whose chalice timidly the tear
perchance will glisten that your loved one shed
on your departure, bidding you farewell.

The journey's end is in the grave, for in
the grave the flame irrevocably dies
that in the cloister of your spirit burned.

And yet within that mansion at whose door
our breath is quenched, there breathes another breath
by which we are awaked to life anew.

There an end is made of strength and talent,
there an end is made of pain and pleasure,
there an end is made of faith and feeling,

there an end is made of earthly joys,
and the idiot and the sage together
sink to the abode where all are equal.

Yet in that same place where the soul is spent
and spent the body, in that selfsame place
the dying being is a nascent being.

The powerful and fecundating pit
annexes to itself the being that was
and from it draws and shapes the being to be.

To unforgiving history it abandons
a name, indifferent and unconcerned
whether it die or whether it endure.

It receives the clay and it alone,
and, altering its form and destiny,
ensures that it shall live eternally.

The grave holds nothing but a skeleton;
and life within this mortuary vault
continues secretly to find its substance.

For when this transient existence ends
to which with such solicitude we cling,
matter, immortal as glory, is endowed
with other semblances, but never dies.

Salvador Díaz Mirón (1853–1928)

1

Grief

Escorted by two policemen, little doubting
they guard and quiet a ferocious monster,
I arrive, saluted by heart-rending
cries and clutched by epileptic arms.

I halt trembling and speechless on the threshold.
A long thick taper reveals and aggravates
with faint gleam the horrible retreat.
The flame flickers in the draught, slant and yellow. . . .
From the wick it strives to wrench itself
and flee the misery that it slavish lights!

On the wretched and funereal bed,
in a black garment alien of aspect,
the hands joined together on the breast,
ice on the belly and a cloth over the face,
stiff and motionless the body lies.

And before this form in which my father
was I weep, in vain by reason admonished
that a corpse is no demolished throne
nor broken altar, but an empty gaol.

What friend does not accompany and support me?
The multitude, entering unasked,
turns about the pallet of death, lamenting;
and in the nearby church the trumpet sounds,
dismal and slow, farewell to the freedman.

For the people the bard is grace, not cark.
He is as the magnolia of the bourne
that rises white and triumphant into view
and to the dust of the way restores and yields
the noble chalice and the goodly scent.

Oh mind that rose and did attain unto
the eminent extreme of your desire!
For what reason did you rail at fate
in accents of the most exceeding grief?

Woe is me, in the waste land standstill,
frenzied, and with half my course to run,
who aspire and strive to cross a river
and find no bridge, nor boat, nor shallow place;
and yonder I discern, among the tilths
of the far bank, the felicitous goal,
and the sun dying, in triumphal honour,
beneath a gold and purple canopy!

I hear a wit say of my destiny:
"An attractive talent; lost however
in the gloom of evil and oblivion. . . .
A precious pearl in the slaver of a mollusc
shut up in its shell and fathoms deep
in a dark and a tempestuous sea. . . ."

In sublime absorption I excite
my mind, with consternation meditate
on that passing of all stars to a West
which yonside an illusion proves an Orient. . . .
And rapturous and reverent I bow me down.

                              (Veracruz, January 4th, 1895)

2

The Corpse

Like the bole of a fallen mountain tree.
A clear, majestic, pure and lofty brow.
Black brows together drawn in the fine
and arching line that images the flight

of a bird lightly sketched against the sky.
Nostrils like a falcon's beak. Pallor
of ivory hair. Already verdureless
the pine fell and lies, part ringed with hoar.

The eyeball, stretching the ill-sutured lids,
emits a dark and glassy gleam of grief,
sheen of well water over its numbed depths.

With my handkerchief I fright and scatter
flies; and on the dead face a vague shadow
hovers, as of a condor, or of flight.

3

The Example

The corpse rotted from its exhibiting noose
like a horrible fruit from the bough,
witness to an unbelievable sentence,
swaying pendulous above the road.

The obscene nakedness, the protruding tongue,
and a high tuft of hair like a cockscomb,

lent it a comic look; at my horse's feet
a group of rapscallions sported and guffawed.

And the dismal remains, with lolling head,
scandalous and swollen on the green gibbet,
spread their gust of stench upon the breeze,

swinging with a censer's measured gravity.
And the sun rose in the immaculate blue,
and the land was like a poem of Tibullus.

4

The Phantom

White and delicate, like white lilies,
hardly visible among the cloak,
the hands . . . the hands that do not break my chains.

Blue and strewn with a sand of gold,
blue and golden as unclouded nights,
the eyes . . . the eyes that contemplate my sins.

White the neck as the dove's snowy breast,
Beard and hair like to the mane of the sun,
And like to silver the shapely foot unshod.

Mild and sad the face, the garment blue. . . .
Thus across the mighty lake of evil
Jesus came to my unction, as to the bark.

And the pinnacle glittered on my spirit
its fleeting and abundant certitude,
as though with radiance of reflected light.

So he wonts to come and give me back
the faith that saves and the illusion that gladdens,
and for a flash my dark soul is aflame.

5

Nox

No syrup or perfume
is like your prattle....
What spiced and sugared
lozenge in
your mouth will melt
its honey and amber
when oh virgin alone
with me you speak?

Your marriage-feast
will be to-morrow.

To the glory of night
you turn your face,
fairer than the roses
at the window;
and your golden tresses
stream on the breeze
and your troubled face
chances to move me....

Your marriage-feast
will be to-morrow.

On a cabal a comet
pounces in the gloom.

It is a weeping emblem,
a sign of song.
Point and stroke
compose the star;
it figures a note,
depicts a tear.

Your marriage-feast
will be to-morrow.

Invisible flock,
the cranes pass over,
beating high
their mighty wings;
dismal, harsh,
they cry and rail,
as if bewailing
a disaster.

Your marriage-feast
will be to-morrow.

A hovering cloudlet,
rising, falling,
languid, flaccid,
solemn, white,
feigns in doubly
symbolic aspect
the bridal veil,
the winding-sheet.

Your marriage-feast
will be to-morrow.

By the gauze that takes
on magic form,
Scorpio queries,

while his alpha
is budding crimson,
bleeding portent. . . .
And love and grief
whet separate arms!

Your marriage-feast
will be to-morrow.

Ah! would the vile earth
that through the vast
abysses wheels
its slavish track
might end its rounds
and be dispelled,
dissolved in wisps
of tenuous rack.

Your marriage-feast
will be to-morrow.

The sea's faint wave
stirs on the shore,
flooding, drowning
nor peoples nor aught.
Of Sodom's fire
I see no ember,
and the red arrow
of lightning is quivered.

Your marriage-feast
will be to-morrow.

Ah Tirsa! already
the hour and my heart
misgives and my soul
in a lark's trill is flown.

Dawn unfolds
her nacreous veil
and Lucifer raises
his pale pearl.

6

To an Araucaria

Hail to you, green hymn, that in superb
and starry rhymes exalt your glorious
divinity and stir the soul to song!

On the rigidly prolific peak
of your elegant and plumy spire
a garrulous blackbird sobs his welladay.

And I spread Parnassian wing and toss
it on the wild wind of the rugged Cofre,
and salute you with barbaric measure.

In guise of foliage, bifid tipped, you crook
your prongs, menacing, as from the tails
of some unheard of breed of savage snakes.

And if the flames of rancour hem about
my heart and lute, the music is rebuke
and the verse a claw imbrued with blood.

What outlandishness in your fresh fronds!
The garlands that you lift up to the clouds
are a lode before the eyes, a spell upon them.

I too am alien, and more of cynosure
with the fame I vaunt, the insults I expunge,
and from a loftier estate I fall.

You swoon enfolded in miraculous light
and a trembling iridescence of tears
diamonds and impearls your diadems.

I burn in an oestrus of love, no dew
like it that lies upon the anguishes
I send to God and that my angel heals.

Engraved in you in you my name is mingled!
It may be in your keeping it will not perish!
Through you alone it can endure and grow!

7

Within an Emerald

Beside the sycamore, in hesitating
maiden trembling, you unclasp your smock.
On the gay margin of the laughing stream
I wait for the loose covering to fall.

And there, spreading its coif towards your hair,
a leaf that seems of glass in the May sun
turns green the light of the refulgent ray,
imbedding you in an enormous gem.

Modesty in a virgin is a buckler;
and on your charms, no sooner bared, you loose
a prudent and abundant torrent of splendours.

You unbraid a cataract of curls,
and peerless tresses cover peerless beauty
and with their tips caress your flower-like feet.

Manuel José Othón (1858–1906)

1

A Steppe in the Nazas Country

No trace of verdant hillside, nor of meadow.
There is nothing, nothing before my eyes,
nothing save the burning desiccated
endless plain where spring has never reigned.

In the gloomy bowl the monotonous river
rolls, with never a rapid, never a gorge,
and, low on the horizon, the setting sun
reverberates, like a furnace mouth.

And here in this grisaille that never is
lit up by any colour, here where the air
scourges the scorched plant with fiery breath,

alone the cotton, breaking from its prison,
in the strawy plantations loftily
proclaims the white note of its candid plume.

2

Elegy

I

Along the tangled path and in the red
mountain and in the monotonous plain

there survives not a trace of verdure,
not a blade of grass, not a thistle.

Alone from the obscure latania
the arid ivy hangs its last remains
above the murmur of the south-west wind
and the rustling heaps of stubble straw.

Evening falls cinereous and chill
and over the homestead and the sea
an overwhelming desolation spreads.

There is no sound of life save, at the hour
of the most sorrowful decline of day,
the ashen crane crying among the fallows.

II

What depth of sadness over all the scene!
At the destroying breath of the cold north
all movement was suspended in the fields
and the branches and the trunks made moan.

There are no more nests, nor songs, nor leaves,
not a murmur, not a voice is heard,
and the wild goose, by the trembling lake,
with its croaking scarcely breaks the still.

In the regions where Aquilon lets loose
its fury and with clamour rushes headlong,
ceaseless, ceaseless are the frost and rain;

While the sepulchral whiteness of the snow
immensely spreads and ever further spreads,
hope-destroying, tragic, infinite.

III

If such might of frozen solitude
holds in thralls the sea and earth and sky,
if the limpid brook has ceased to flow
and the rose to sway upon the mead,

ah! let us not think that life expires:
in the winding-sheet of its white veil,
beneath the opaque crystal of the ice,
immortal resurrection is in store.

But what ear can catch the mysterious
voices that with mystic murmur rise
from out the most hidden womb of things?

Nothing perishes: the buried germ,
the chrysalis enveloped in its sheath,
the cell and the grain . . . all are sleeping!

3

Wild Idyll

I

What brought you to my frozen solitude,
overshadowed by the dying rack
of a grey twilight? . . . Behold the scene,
arid, sad, immeasurably sad.

If you come from sorrow, if your heart
on sorrow feeds, I bid you welcome to

the savage wilderness, where scarce a mirage
of that which was my youth remains behind.

But if perchance you come from less afar
and in your soul the taste of pleasure lingers,
better return to your tumultuous world.

If not, come and dip your Cyprian mantle
in the bittermost unfathomed sea
of grievous love or of exceeding tears.

II

Behold the scene: immensity below,
immensity, immensity above;
the high sierra bulking against the sky,
its base eroded with a dreadful cleft.

Gigantic boulders, torn by the earthquake
from the entrails of the living rock;
and throughout that brooding and adust
savannah, not a path, not a track.

Devastating incandescent air
where the serene imbedded eagles are
like nails being slowly driven home.

Awesomeness of silence, gloom, appal,
broken only, scarcely broken, by
the exultant gallop of the dappled deer.

III

In the accursed steppe, beneath the thrust
of the murderous sibilating blast,
you raise your delicate and sculptural form
like a relief imprinted on its verge.

The wind, labouring among the dunes,
sings with the voice of a celestial music
and imitates, beneath the drenching mist,
an infinite and solitary kiss.

In the fading light your eyes discharge
a dart dark with passion and distress
that fastens in my spirit and my flesh;

and, flagrant against the dying sun,
like a crest of plumes, immensely streaming,
your long black hair, your wild Indian's hair.

IV

The salt and infinitely bitter plain,
like a dead ocean's desiccated bed,
and, in the grey distance, by way of haven,
the precipitous crags, forsaken and stark.

On my rigid face the evening spreads,
like unguent, horrible obscurity,
and on your skin, burnt by the sun, the copper
and sepia of the wilderness's rocks.

And in the hollow where eternal shadow,
beneath the craggy peaks' enormous frown,
provides a bower and cavern for our love,

the lianas of your body twine
about the virile subjugating trunk
in a vast palpitation of our lives.

V

What morbid grievous infinity of distance!
What sullen and inexorable flatness!

Such horror hovers over all the scene
as on a place steeped in the blood of slaughter.

And the shadow that lengthens, lengthens, lengthens,
seems, with its tragic swathes, as though it were
the mighty spirit, full of bitterness,
of those doomed in hopelessness to die.

And there we tarry, with the overwhelming
sense of the affliction of all the passions,
beneath the weight of all the oblivions.

In a leaden sky the sun already
dead; and in our lacerated hearts
the desert and the desert and the desert!

VI

So farewell! . . . Yonder, austere and dark,
you retreat across the sun-scorched plain,
and all down your shoulders your ardent tresses,
verberating, like a malediction.

In my desolation what awaits me? . . .
—already I scarce can see your dragging skirt—
a drifting down of spring's young foliage
and endless longing for emerald past and gone.

The human cataclysm has destroyed
my heart and all expires that it holds . . .
perish memory and oblivion perish!

I glimpse you still and already forget your brow;
your back alone alas! I see, as that
is seen which flees eternity and recedes.

Envoy

On your altars I have spent my incense,
shed my last remaining roses' petals.
Where the shrines of my goddesses arose
is nothing now but a vast waste of sand.

I sought to enter your soul, and what a fall,
what a wildering midst ruins and pits!
To such things I have given so much thought
that all my thought is pain and thought of pain.

Ended! . . . And what remains of such exceeding
rapture? In you neither moral grief
nor aftertaste of lust, nor taste of tears.

In me what deep and dreadful cataclysm!
What darkness in my conscience and what dread,
and what a nausea of self-disgust!

Manuel Gutiérrez Nájera (1859–1895)

1

Dead Waters

In the dark beneath the earth
where no eye has ever probed,
silent streams of water slide
in a never-ending course.
The uppermost, surprised at last
by the rock-transpiercing steel,

limpid and ebullient spring
in a mighty plume of spray.
But the others deep in gloom
ever tortuously glide
in the unavailing quest
for vent, doomed to flow for ever.

To the sea the rivers wend,
in their shifting silver glass
mirroring the stars of heaven
or the pallid hues of dawn;
they are clad in veils of flowers,
naiads in their waters bathe,
they fecundate the fertile vales
and their waves are liquid song.

In the snowy marbled fountain
gay and playful the water as
a little girl in a royal palace
scattering her chains of pearls.
Now like a dark arrow it springs,
now feathers like an open fan;
it strews the leaves with diamonds
and lulls itself with murmured song.

In the sovereign sea the waves
beat on the precipitous rocks;
turbulent they shake the earth
and in tumult scale the skies.
There water is life and dauntless might,
there it is the ireful king,
it joins with heaven in equal strife
and contends with gods and monsters.

How different is the black wave
condemned to a perpetual prison,
it that dwells beneath the earth,

too deep even for the stark dead!
It that never felt the light,
it that never sobs nor sings,
it mute and known to none,
it blind and held a slave!

Even as it, known to none,
even as it, deep in gloom,
so are you likewise, you obscure
and silent waters of my soul.
Who has ever traced your course?
None pitying descends to look
upon you. And deep, deep down,
your captive silent flood extends.
Given outlet you would gush
like the bubbling waterspout
that rears its furious column of foam
higher than the pines and cedars.
But imprisoned you will never,
never know the light of day.
Roll on in the dark for ever,
silent waters of my soul!

2

To Be

A fathomless abyss is human pain.
Whose eye has ever pierced to its black depths?
To the shadowy gulf of times that are
no more incline your ear. . . .
                              Within there falls
the eternal tear!
                   To the defenceless mouths
that in another age life such as ours

inspired, curious draw nigh. . . .
                          A groan
arises trembling from the whitened bones!

Life is pain. And life persists, obscure,
but life for all that, even in the tomb.
Matter disintegrates and is dispersed;
the eternal spirit, the underlying
essence suffers without pause. It were
in vain to wield the suicidal steel.
Suicide is unavailing. The form
is changed, the indestructible being endures.

In thee, Pain, we live and have our being!
The supreme yearning of all existing things
is to be lost in nothingness, annulled,
deep in dreamless sleep. . . . And life continues
beyond the frozen confines of the tomb.

There is no death. In vain you clamour for death,
souls destitute of hope. And the implacable
purveyor of suffering creatures ravishes
us to another world. There is no pause.
We crave a single instant of respite
and a voice in the darkness urges: "On!"

Yes, life is an evil and an evil
that never ends. The creating God
is the creature of another terrible God
whose name is Pain. And the immortal
Saturn is insatiate. And space,
the nursery of suns, the infinite,
are the mighty prison, issueless,
of souls that suffer and that cannot die.

Oh implacable Saturn, make an end
at last, devour created things and then,

since we are immortal, ruminate our lives!
We are thine, Pain, thine for evermore,
but pity for the beings that are not yet,
save in thy mind that hunger stimulates....
Pity, oh God, have pity on nothingness!
At last be sated, that the eternal womb,
begetter of the seed of humankind,
turn barren and that life come to an end....
And let the world like a dead planet whirl
amid the waveless oceans of the void!

3

Fragment from "Pax Anima"

To remember ... To forgive ... To have loved ...
To be an instant happy, to have believed ...
And then in weariness to lean upon
the snowy shoulder of oblivion.

To feel eternally the tenderness
that palpitates within our youthful breasts,
and, like the visit of a lovely woman,
to receive good fortune, if it comes.

Ever hidden that which we love most;
ever on our lips the smiling pardon;
until at last, oh earth! to thee we go
with the invincible lassitude of sleep.

So he must live who meditates upon
the fleetingness of all that he beholds,
and forbears, wise, before the vast
extension of thy seas, oh Falsity!

He gathers flowers, as long as there are flowers;
he grants the rose forgiveness of its thorns. . . .
And this even though the air be dark
with the black butterflies of thronging sorrow.

He loves and forgives, with courage strives
against the unjust, the ignoble and the coward. . . .
In melancholy and in pensiveness
beautifully falls the silent evening!

When the shadow of pain is on my spirit
I seek brightness on the heights, and calm,
and an infinite compassion dawns
on the frozen summits of my soul!

4

Non Omnis Moriar

Dear heart, I shall not altogether die.
Something of my elusive scattered spirit
shall within the line's diaphanous urn
by Poetry be piously preserved.

I shall not altogether die; when stricken
I fall beneath the blows of human pain,
you will make haste and from the shadowy
battlefield raise up the dying brother.

It may be then, from the vanquished mouth,
mute and aspiring the infinite calm,
that to your ears will come the voice of all
that sleeps with open eyes within my soul.

Deep buried memories of fleeting days;
the solitary sighs of melancholy
tenderness; and pallid ailing joys
sobbing to the music of the viols.

All that the man hides fearfully away
will from the poet, vibrant, issue forth
in golden measures of secret orison
whose every period invokes your name.

And you will perhaps observe that in strange wise
my verses sound on your attentive ear,
and in the glass I sully with my breath
will contemplate the image of my thought.

Seeing then what I was wont to dream,
of my faltering poetry you will say:
gloomy and vulgar were his songs of old,
but this, now, how beautiful it was!

Because I shrine your memory in strains
of the living, sacred, universal quire;
because the gleam of unfamiliar tears
shines in the bitter chalice of my hymn;

because blest Poetry exists and you
in it irradiate, in that same verse
that holds a scattered atom of my being,
dear heart, I shall not altogether die!

5

When the Day Comes

I want to die with the dying day,
on the high sea and with my face to the sky,

where the pangs of death may seem a dream
and the soul a mew on soaring wing.

At the last, to hear no other voice,
alone already with the sky and sea,
no other voice, no other sobbing knell,
than the mighty heaving of the deep.

To die when the melancholy light
withdraws its golden nets from the green waves,
and be as yonder slowly expiring sun,
a thing of exceeding brightness, perishing.

To die, and young; before the pleasant crown
is brought to nothing by perfidious time;
while life, although we know full well she is
a traitoress, still says: "I am thine."

Francisco A. de Icaza (1863–1925)

1

Responding Voice

Our life is not life, save in the fleeting
moments wrested from the barren task
of the daily struggle's paltry fray
that in its sameness likens men to brutes.

Our life is not life, save in the intense
instant that whips the flesh like a lightning flash,
that floods the spirit with the light of stars
and burns and strews it like a grain of incense.

2

Wayfaring

Sing! Why should I sing,
drawn unwillingly
by devious ways
I must retrace?
Sing! Why should I sing? . . .

3

Golden

Beneath the evening gold,
above the golden corn,
the mill moves slow
its jagged sails.

Above the golden corn
hugely it shovels down
from sky to earth
the evening hoard.

4

For the Poor Blind Man

Woman, give him alms,
for in life there is nothing
so terrible as being
eyeless in Granada.

Luis G. Urbina (1868–1934)

1

The Ancient Tear

As in the depths of an ancient cavern
lost in the recesses of the mountain,
silently, these centuries, a drop
of water falls;
so in my dark and solitary heart,
in the most hidden secret of my vitals,
I have heard, this long time past, a tear
slowly falling.
What dark cranny filters it to me?
From what mysterious springs does it distil?
To what fertile torrent is it faithless?
From what far source is it to me consigned?
Who knows? . . . When I was a child my tears
were the celestial dew that morning sheds;
when I was a youth they were a storm-cloud,
a tempest of passion and a rain of anguish.
Later, in a wintry eventide,
my tears were snowfall. . . .
Now I weep no more . . . my life is arid
and my soul serene.
And yet . . . why do I feel the dropping thus,
tear after tear,
of some exhaustless spring of tenderness,
some indefatigable vein of grief?
Who knows! . . . It is not I, but those who were
my sad progenitors; it is my race;
the afflicted spirits,
the flagellated flesh;
age-long panting after the impossible,

mystic hopes,
sudden and unbridled melancholy,
ineffectual and savage anger.
In me at my begetting human suffering
left its marks,
its cries, its blasphemies, its supplications.
My heritage it is that weeps, my heritage,
in the depths of my soul.
The grief of my ancestors in my heart
collects, as in a chalice, tear by tear.
So I shall pass it on, when the day comes,
when from the seemly womb of the beloved,
kisses made incarnate, other beings,
transformations of my life, proceed.
I am at my desk. The afternoon
is kindly. My room is bright with sun.
Outside, in the garden, I hear the voices
of the children, their laughter and their singing.
And I think: unhappy creatures, perhaps
already, at this hour of merriment,
in your blithe hearts there seeps, unknown to you,
silent and tenacious, the ancient tear! . . .

2

The Centaur's Bath

The water clangs, the crystal flies in shivers
and he goes down; and of the fiery colt
alone emerge the tawny sculptural head
and the rider's swart and muscled torse.

The waves roll back, biting against the banks,
with convulsive and tumultuous shudder,
and man and beast, in simple and heroic
attitudes, begin a furious struggle.

A smiling nymph, red and firm of flesh,
with lank hair and primitive visage, bathes;
and waters like a girdle clasp her waist;

and she goes unashamed . . . and her breast trembles
with desire to give herself, voluptuous
and wild, to the dark centaur's rude caresses.

3

Dayspring

Whiteness of faintly roseate milk. A line
of azure blanches imperceptibly
the grey of the horizon. The sea seems
an inundation of the sap of lilies.

Mantling the serene and candid clouds
a timid blush extends its radiance,
and on the celestial carmine blooms
the iris of a morning star. Whitely
a hut looms amid the verdurous gloom;
a fringe of foam glitters on the sands,
splendour of golden yellow brightens and spreads,
light triumphant breaks free from its chains
and blazes forth in crimson. It is the dayspring.

4

The Silent Day

The limpid shimmering sea is like a turquoise:
indigo afar, crystal near the shore.

The sun, gently kissing the horizon,
shines on the waters as a mist of gold.

The boat moves gaily to the urging oars;
the surface shivers with a silvery splash;
and neath the mountain, thick with arid green,
a radiant yellow stretch of shore extends.

A pelican, flapping down with fainting flight,
on the deep velvet carpet of the waves
tapers its wings and spreads them open wide.

No sound, no plaint, no anguish, no desire;
life, in love with heaven's opal, swoons
in light-intoxicated lethargy.

5

Our Lives Are Rivers

I had but one illusion—a pleasant fancy:
that of the river drawing to the sea
and yearning to be changed into a pool
an instant, and sleep in some old palm-tree's shade.

And my soul said: I go troubled and weary
of ranging plains and leaping over dikes;
now the storm is past; I need to rest,
to be azure as of old and murmur a song.

I had but one illusion, so serene
that it cured my ills and gladdened my affliction
with the bright gleam of a fire on the hearth.

And life: Soul, go troubled and alone,
no iris on your bank, no star in your wave,
range the plains and vanish in the sea.

Francisco González León (1868?–1945)

Hours

Evenings of beatitude,
even the book forgotten,
because the soul dissolves
lapped in quietude.

Evenings when every
sound lies sleeping.

Evenings when the least
seem anaesthetized,
all the garden flowers,
shadow more shadowy
and the old manor more deserted.

Evenings when the least
creak of furniture
were a profanation
of absurd cacophony
and impious intrusion.

Evenings when the house's
door is fast closed
and the soul's open.

Evenings when the quiet
vane on the steeple

turns, numbed, no more,
and, entire like perfume,
silence is inbreathed.

Amado Nervo (1870–1919)

1

An Old Burden

Who is yonder siren so distressed
of voice, so white of flesh, so dark of tress?
—A ray of moon bathing in the fountain,
a ray of moon. . . .

Who roams the house, crying out my name?
Who calls me in the nights so tremulously?
—A flurry of wind moaning in the tower,
a flurry of wind.

Who art thou, say, archangel, thou whose wings
flame in the evening's divine fire, thou
who soarest through air's glory?
—The passing clouds:
see, mere clouds.

Who dipped in water, God, her necklaces?
Rain of diamonds on azure velvet.
—The image of the sky trembling in the stream,
the image of the sky.

Lord! beauty then is nought but mirage, nought.
Thou art sure: be thou my ultimate Lord.
Where find thee, in the air, on earth, in me?
—A glimmer of dream will guide thee in every abyss,
a glimmer of dream.

2

Evocation

From the deep mystery of the past I called her,
where she is a shadow among shadows,
a vestige among vestiges, a phantom
among phantoms.
And she came to my call,
scattering peoples, spurning centuries.

Dismayed, the laws of time surrounded her;
the spirit of the grave, with dismal clamour,
cried to her: Bide! With invisible clutch
the epochs seized her faded furbelow.

But all in vain! Her red tresses streaming,
red tresses redolent of eternity,
that alien queen, in raiment of chimera,
came hastening to the beck of my desire.

When she was by me I bespoke her thus:
What of thy promise of the year a thousand?
—Mark I am mere shadow.—I know.—Was mad.
—What of thy promised kiss?—Death froze it.—Queens
forswear not! . . .
                    And she kissed me on the mouth.

3

Entreaty to the Cloud

The swan bears on its neck the initial of sleep,
and like a strange white dreaming sleep it passes;

but stranger is the cloud that goes on fire
in the grave sunset and the smiling dawn!

Cloud, visible wake of invisible wind,
thou swan at dawn, raven in the void of night;
cloud, akin to the celestial vane,
cloud, thou ocean and wave and foam and sail!

Cloud, be my protectress. Stoop in pity,
clothe in transfigurations all my doubting,
all the darkness that is in my mind.
As I have sorrowed let me shine, although
the storm wind gather that will strip me bare.

4

And Thou, Expectant . . .

Fraught with stars the dark nights come and go
and come and go the dazzling coral days
and the grey of the rains and the fleeting clouds
. . . and thou, expectant.

Thou expectant and the lingering hours!
How languidly they stir, the torpid plants!
It seems the four-and-twenty sisters are shod
with clogs of lead.

This incandescent rose impends already
within the verdant clusters of its bodice.
Within the verdant clusters the wonder lurks
of its sacred flesh.

But when shall we behold the open rose!
Eternal God, thou never makest haste,
but man is anxious, being ephemeral.
Lord, when shall we behold the open rose!

José Juan Tablada (1871–1945)

1

Haiku *of a Day*

I

Tender willow,
almost gold, almost amber,
almost light. . . .

II

The geese on their
clay trumpets sound
false alarms.

III

Royal peacock, slowly fulgurant,
through the democratic barnyard
you pass like a procession. . . .

IV

Although he never stirs from home
the tortoise, like a load of furniture,
jolts down the path.

V

The garden is thick with dry leaves:
on the trees I never saw
so many green, in spring. . . .

VI

Lumps of mud, the toads
along the shady path
hop. . . .

VII

The bat, in the night,
essays the swallow's flight
so as to fly by day. . . .

VIII

Restore to the bare bough,
nocturnal butterfly,
the dry leaves of your wings!

IX

The nightingale beneath
the awe of heaven raves
its psalm to the sole star.

X

The brilliant moon
working through its web
keeps the spider awake.

XI

Sea the black night,
the cloud a shell,
the moon a pearl.

2

Haiku *of the Flowerpot*

I

The multicoloured mushroom seems
a Japanese toad's
parasol.

II

The dragon-fly strives patiently
to fasten its transparent cross
to the bare and trembling bough.

III

Ants on inert cricket crawling.
Memory
of Gulliver in Lilliput.

IV

Mingled, in the quiet evening,
chimes of angelus and bats
and swallows fly.

V

The little fly-tormented ass,
while he is being burdened, dreams
of emerald Elysian Fields. . . .

VI

The tiny monkey looks at me. . . .
He would like to tell me something
that escapes his mind!

VII

Beneath my window the moon on the roofs,
and the cats' silhouettes,
and their Chinese music.

VIII

Amidst the blue and white waves
the rolling swim of dolphins,
arabesques of wings and anchors.

IX

Smitten by the solar sun
the glass sea breaks to shivers.

X

The clock seems gnawing at the midnight feast,
echoed by the rat's
minute-hand.

XI

Red cold
guffaw of summer,
slice
of watermelon!

3

Dawn in the Cockloft

Cocks in the north at dawn
crow softly, drowsily.

Cocks in the south
crow when the stars
of dawn are grains of maize
in the sky's wide blue close.

Clarion. Clangour.
Every clarion clamant
for the supreme clarion cry.

Cockloft dian,
dawn stir
of cavalry.

At night when the last
fortress is ashes,
dreaming we hear
blue rockets soar,
violet and white,
when the cocks crow. . . .

In your insomnia, festive spirit,
do you not hear him crowing,
the cock who flung to heaven the doubloons
of the Seven of Gold? . . .

Gazing on this night gambling soon I saw,
falling through the blackness of space,
in golden dust and topaz mist
the four notes of the cockalorum. . . .

Symphonic cockloft,
across your harsh and strident clarions
a neigh of terror peals,
runaway, like a colt,
and, murmurous, the other sounds,
household, rural,
of the village morning,
light as running water. . . .

4

The Idol in the Porch

On the morning
sky a stone of sun
shows its broad basalt
face on high
at the edge of a pool of obsidian,
and the mouth seems to pour
dribble of human blood
and helianthi of death. . . .

It is the great grindstone
of the solar corn

that makes the bread of days
in the mills of eternity.

Stone of chronologies,
synthesis of years and days,
breathing in silent song
the unconquerable dread
of old mythologies. . . .
On it the flowered and divining months
string pallid alabaster moons
like hollow skulls on the *zompantli*
in the temple.

About this Table of the Law
the months assemble, mystic, sworded,
in warlike song, murmur of prayer,
as about a King. . . .

And at the close of the belated days
the Nemontani. . . . Five, in masks,
with thistly aloe-leaves!

Days in whose nights the moon
dissolves like turbid chalchuite,
days when shadow-stained the sun gold shines
like tiger-skin, like sunflower. . . .

Like the Tropic other days
are rich and sonorous, and when the jaguar roars
and clouds of parakeets arise
it is as though the forest took to wing.

And the flash of the macaws
sears the sky—clamour and oriflamme—
and gleam and echo seem
flung by the legion of the God of Battles.

And in broad day the quetzels' tails
soar and whirl like Catherine wheels,
like showering stars, flying flowers,
fountains of emerald, gushing, falling
in sprays of willow. . . .

The great anaconda writhes
like sinuous water,
and the thicket quivers
its vast bulk, cold and chill,
inlaid with flowers, encrusted with stars,
in strict geometry.

Other evenings the wild herds of bison
pour across the plain,
their humps rolling like hills
or stormy sea asurge with billows.

In the tall bamboo the macaws screech;
with dreadful crunching,
trailing havoc,
an earthquake plunges through the brake:
the Tapir.

The iguana has changed the sunflower of its iris
and the armadillo fled
to hiding in its carapace.
Huddled in its shell, wound in a ball,
it rolled through the mountain all night and day
and safe to the valley came.

From the azure where it hovered
the pursuing eagle
deemed it dead. . . .
And soon the armadillo, like a holy
desert hermit, rose into the sun.

It escaped the eagle's claw,
but in the end changed into a guitar
beneath a southern
Zapatist's hand
full of patriot love
of the Promised Land,
the armadillo at the foot
of the Idol of the Porch
sings the song.

5

The Parrot

Parrot identical with that
of grandmother, grotesque voice
of kitchen, corridor and terrace.

With the first rays of the sun
the parrot breaks into his cry
and into his bitter song,
to the sparrow's consternation
who only sings *El Josefito*. . . .

Choleric and gutteral
he makes little of the cook,
apostrophizing as he goes
the pot of hotch.

When the parrot, treading on
my feet, traverses the brick floor,
the black cat, curled up in a ball,
fixes him with amber eye,
glowering diabolic sulphur
at this green and yellow demon,
nightmare of its somnolence.

But treasures of civilization
appertain unto
the voice of this super-parrot
of 1922.

Hum of aeroplane it parrots
and the claxon's stridency. . . .
And squawking seeks to overcome
the Victor pick-up's rival strains. . . .

Golden spotlight on a little stage,
from beams to floor, corner to corner,
a sunray through the kitchen strays,
blinds and nimbs the strutting bird. . . .

But sometimes, when the goldfinch breaks
into the song of April woods,
then the prating parrot's sudden
silence and rapt sidelong gaze
are eloquent of a melancholy
unworthy of his green and plumes. . . .

Perhaps he recalls the mighty forest
and the thicket's shadowy bowl. . . .

To the cook according truce
he suspends his scurrilous chatter
and lapses into a wild gloom. . . .

The parrot is but a tuft of leaves
and on the pate a patch of sun.

6

Alternating Nocturne

Golden New York night,
cold limedark walls,

Rector's, foxtrot, champagne,
    still houses, strong bars,
and looking back,
    above the silent roofs,
the spirit petrified,
    the white cats of the moon,
like Lot's wife.

And yet
    it is one,
        at New York,
            at Bogota,
                and the same
                    moon!

Enrique González Martínez (1871–1952)

1

Wring the Swan's Neck

Wring the swan's neck who with deceiving plumage
inscribes his whiteness on the azure stream;
he merely vaunts his grace and nothing feels
of nature's voice or of the soul of things.

Every form eschew and every language
whose processes with deep life's inner rhythm
are out of harmony . . . and greatly worship
life, and let life understand your homage.

See the sapient owl who from Olympus
spreads his wings, leaving Athene's lap,
and stays his silent flight on yonder tree.

His grace is not the swan's, but his unquiet
pupil, boring into the gloom, interprets
the secret book of the nocturnal still.

2

When It Is Given You to Find a Smile

When it is given you to find a smile
in the tenuous drop of moisture by
the porous stone distilled, in the mist,
in the sun, in the bird and in the wind;

when nothing to your eyes remains inert,
or formless, or colourless, or remote,
and when you penetrate the mystery
and the life of silence, dark and death;

when to the different courses of the cosmos
your gaze extends, and your own effort is
the effort of a powerful microscope
bringing into view invisible worlds;

then in the blazing conflagration of
an infinite and superhuman love,
with the Saint of Assisi you will say
brother to tree and cloud and savage beast.

You will feel in the unnumbered throng
of things and beings the being that is yours;
you will be all terror with the abyss
and with the summit you will be all pride.

The ignoble dust will stir your love
that maculates the whiteness of the lily,

your blessing will be on the sandy beaches,
your adoration for the insect's flight;

and you will kiss the talon of the thorn
and the dahlia's silken draperies. . . .
And you will piously put off your sandals
in order not to bruise the wayside stones.

3

House with Two Doors

Oh house with two doors that is mine,
vast and shadowy dwelling of the heart,
that in the years' procession I have seen
full sometimes of strange guests
and almost empty other times—the most!

House that in
life's smiling instants contemplated rapt
the interminable flow of dreams,
not slow to come, not slow to go again.

How few the travellers who on their departure
left, for future passers by this way,
a fire burning
at the goodly door by which they went
or a noble inscription on the walls!

Mostly they left, in the uncertain radiance
of an untimely sundown,
some rag behind on the deserted threshold,
the wandering soul of some dead song of praise
or a wornness of stone beneath their tread.

Alone in the silence and the peace
of night, an unknown guest suspends
his quiet lamp. . . .
And my faint-spirited disquiet wonders
if it is a weary love arriving
late or an old sorrow not yet gone.

4

Pain

Its gaze filled my abyss, its gaze melted
into my being, became so mine that I
am doubtful if this breath of agony
is life still or hallucinated death.

The archangel came, cast his sword
upon the double laurel flourishing
in the sealed garden. . . . And that day brought back
the shadow and I returned to my nothingness.

I thought the world, witnessing man's appal,
would crumble, overwhelmed beneath the ruins
of the entire firmament crashing down.

But I saw the earth at peace, at peace the heavens,
the fields serene, limpid the running stream,
blue the mountain and the wind at rest.

5

The Condemned

Proffered to sun and moon
on my deserted shore I tell and tell
again the black beads of my destiny.

I am the same who once
entreated of the stars serenity . . .
and here am I, waiting and watching still!

I unwind my silent reel;
I contemplate my past and every hour
blushes for very nakedness as it passes.

Childish apparitions. . . . Was not mine,
in the blue opal of the sleepless dawn,
a swan imbrued with blood of agony?

I blew my bubble high in the unseeing
eddying air, and the untimely blast
shattered the crystal of the rainbow toy.

I let the world into my dream and loved
with love that sheltered in my innocent breast
the snake of doubt and the nightingale of song.

I craved to forge my life in an enormous
forge of love, with bellows of hurricanes,
with my own hands and without thought of **mede;**

or to be stainless snow upon the summit
of the tutelary mount, by nought
save sun and cloud and tempest overtopped;

or to be given in holocaust to the sorrows
of the fraternal herd, and the noble rain
water my blood converted into flowers. . . .

I curbed the urge of such sublime intent
and fed with my humility the flame
of a romantic unassuming ideal:

to be a glittering vase of crystal water
and plunged within it the miraculous stem
of a flower of godlike fashioning;

or to burn like yonder sacred lamp
consuming its sweet-smelling oil within
the alcove of the holy hermitage;

or to be a bird with lyric wiles
beguiling the pilgrim who has lost his way
and mocking at the sortilege of years. . . .

And I launched blindly forth, from rhyme to rhyme,
until at last the tower of my dreams
sundered at its base and overwhelmed me.

Neither laurel branch nor opalescent
halo of sanctity, neither fresh rose
nor noble thorn on my denuded brow.

In my youth I was the furtive fowler
who laid his snare in the forbidden close
to catch the bird of fugitive delights.

My quest was for the glory of the richest
trophy, and my flesh, a ravening wolf,
pursued the colt of runaway desire.

I killed my dream, that I might find the way
to sink my teeth in the envenomed fruit,
and many books made me all-ignorant.

(Evil by life's ironical grimace
is emphasized, and good shamefacedly
like a repentant shadow passes by). . . .

In the dark cavern of my consciousness
great love descended suddenly. . . . A wing
fluttered and to its call my hope arose.

I laid open my heart to her who came
holding a basket of roses in her hand . . .
and on my lips she kissed me, and was mine.

And all my past and all my present turned
to light. . . . One evening it went out and left
my life in the shadow of the departed.

Herd of the winds, high shepherd of the dawns,
beneath the indigo sweep of my lofty plain
I sought a quiet pasture for my hours;

and at the barking of the vigilant dog
the frantic scattering of my lambs remains
deaf to the lamentations of the bell.

I contemplated, the tragic labour ended,
the obliterated furrows and useless grain. . . .
I ploughed the water and I sowed the sand!

And here am I, trembling on the brink
of the solemnly accusing conscience. . . .
An evildoer in terror before himself!

I named me my own judge and I condemned me,
alone and outcast, to the extremest torment:
not to ask forgiveness of my folly
and in the dungeons of silence to end my days.

6

Romance of the Living Corpse

There are hours I imagine
that I am dead;

that I perceive only forms
wound in the shrouds of time;
that I am scarce a phantasm
seen by some in dreams;
that I am a sleepless bird
in its blindness blindly singing;
that I fled thither—I know not when—
whither "she" and "he" departed;
that I seek them, seek
them and see them not,
and that I am a shadow among shadows,
in endless night.

But of a sudden life
dawns on fire
and I hear a voice that calls me,
as before, crying loud;
and thronging desire
at the sight runs riot
and the senses ramp
like ravening lions. . . .
And here, here dwells a soul
so close, so deep within,
that to tear it from my breast
were to tear forth my own. . . .
And I am the same again,
dreaming I am awake
and astride on life
as on an unbridled colt. . . .

You alone, you who came
like a secret gift to me,
you for whom the night sings
and the silence lightens;
you alone, you who came
from your glorious circle's centre
with loving flight

down to my hell;
you alone, while your hands
stray in my hair
and your eyes rest on mine
before the kiss,
you alone can tell me
if I am alive or dead.

7

Last Journey

He has gone
the silent road. He goes
before me. He carries his torch
clear already of the traitorous air.

He goes murmuring the verse he could not say
the last evening.
His smile died and in his eyes
the deep dread trembled of what now he knows.

I call him, follow him. He turns no more
his face to me to say: "father,
here is my youth, I give it up to you,
here is my heart, here is my blood."

When my pursuing steps, by absence quickened,
come up with him,
and we are joined before the burning glass
of time-delivered images,
I shall see his face and see his brow
sink on my breast.

There he and I shall know who sets a day
for the departing, and the journey's why.

Rafael López (1875?–1943)

Venus Poised

Thou art present in my shadowiness
like the flight of a scarlet bird to one
by a grey closing in of evening houseled.

And thine early morning gladness peals
a sonorous efflulgence on my life
with its bell of crystal and of silver

shaken in a hush like that of death,
snatching me from the terror of Good Friday
to the jubilance of flowered Easter.

From its dereliction by the grace
of thy spring's sortilege my head absolved
is in a rose and amaranthine turmoil.

Not otherwise the cloud—a passenger
aboard the ardent vessel of the dawn—
gaudies its pennon's customary pallor.

And the instant once again possesses
the value of that drifting hope that day
labours to grapple to the hour's anchor.

The cajolement of the melody sung
by the marvelling illusion turns
to a crepuscular Hungarian violin.

An entreaty trembles in its throat
towards those pupils changing as the wave
pierced by the Evil One in thy saintly face.

Boldness I command to get to hiding,
feeling to follow to the same retreat,
for all that I possess of thy fair beauty

is a golden sepulchre for my sighs
and a shroud of snow for my desire
—aeroplane on reefs of sapphire wrecked.

I live a miracle; when I behold thee
the hour crumbles away into a second
as the flash into its scintillation.

Life draws me into its deep rhythm, the inner
embers feed a flame, forgotten spring
casts for me its spells upon the world.

Thine anagram is youth and grace and love,
simple, yet too hard for my delirium;
I would be, to disentangle thy web,

gardener in the garden of sweet torments,
hid by an abetting arras of blushes,
in thy lap of roses and of lilies,

on thy mouth of crimson hyacinth,
and a lingering sun of summer splendour
dallying in the ivy of thine eyes.

On a handspan of azure thine impress
alone alleviates my coward dusk,
like the dove of Venus the beautiful
poised on the cornices of evening.

Efrén Rebolledo (1877–1929)

The Vampire

Whirling your deep and gloomy tresses pour
over your candid body like a torrent,
and on the shadowy and curling flood
I strew the fiery roses of my kisses.

As I disenmesh the tangled locks
I feel the light chill chafing of your hand,
and a great shudder courses over me
and penetrates me to the very bone.

Your chaotic and disdainful eyes
glitter like stars when they hear the sigh
that from my vitals issue rendingly,

and you, thirsting, as I agonize,
assume the form of an implacable
black vampire battening on my burning blood.

Manuel de la Parra (1878–1930)

The Well

I know not what is in the well, mother!
If it were the soul!
Last night I went to the abandoned garden:
I entered on the silent
paths now blind with briers,
and I was weary,

more than with the way,
with weariness of soul!

So to the margin of the well I came
where I was wont to sing,
wont to sing joyful songs,
and I stooped to its waters.
Black waters, mother!
Fearful to look upon.
I know not what is in their depths:
they reflect no more, as once, limpid,
radiance of moon or stars'
celestial tears.
For over them the lichen has drawn
its wanton lamentable webs.
I know not what is in the well, mother!
If it were the soul. . . !

Ramón López Velarde (1888–1921)

1

My Cousin Agueda

My godmother invited my cousin
Agueda to spend the day
with us, and my cousin
came with a conflicting
prestige of starch and fearful
ceremonious weeds.

Agueda appeared, sonorous
with starch, and her green eyes

and ruddy cheeks protected
me against the fearsome
weeds.

        I was a small boy,
knew O was the round one,
and Agueda knitting,
mild and persevering,
in the echoing gallery,
gave me unknown shivers.
(I think I even owe her the heroically
morbid habit of soliloquy.)

At dinner-time in the quiet
shadowy dining-room,
I was spellbound by the brittle
intermittent noise of dishes
and the caressing timbre
of my cousin's voice.

        Agueda was
(weeds, green pupils, ruddy cheeks)
a polychromatic basket of
apples and grapes
in the ebony of an ancient cupboard.

2

In the Wet Shadows

On the dark wings of the cutting blast
you bring me at the same time pain and joy;
something like a soft breast's frozen virtue,
something that combines the cordial cool
and icy forlornness of a virgin's bed.

And lo, in the mute city's unlooked for gloom,
you are a light before the murky fauces
of my hunger; lo, in the rain's wet shadow
you exude candour like new-washed linen
and, like it, spread an odour of chastity;
lo, in the darkness you distil the essence
of some good fiancée's tearful handkerchief.

I huddle in the thick obscurity
and think for you these lines whose hidden rhyme
you must with rapid divination mark;
for they are petals of night that bring you tidings
of singular thrill; and plunged within my self
in the wet shadows, I send confusedly
these fragile syllables, like a gust of mystery,
to the threshold of your vigilant spirit.

You are all shed upon me like white frost,
and the translucent meteor continues
out of time; and your far words within
me sound with the dreamlike intensity
of a disordered clock striking all hours
in a disordered room. . . .

3

Now, as Never . . .

Now, as never, you fill me with love and sorrow;
if any tear is left me, I quicken it
to wash our two obscurities.

Now, as never, I need your presiding peace;
yet already your throat is but a whiteness

of suffering, suffocating, coughing, coughing,
and your whole being but a screed of dying strokes
overflowing with dramatic farewells.

Now, as never, your essence is venerable
and frail your body's vase, and you can give
me only the exquisite affliction of
a clock of agonies, ticking for us towards
the icy minute when the feet we love
must tread the ice of the funereal boat.

From the bank I watch you embark; the silent
river sweeps you away, and you distil
within my soul the climate of those evenings
of wind and dust when only the church-bells chime.

My spirit is a cloth of souls, a cloth
of souls of an eternally needy church,
it is a cloth of souls bedabbled with wax,
trampled and torn by the ignoble herd.

I am but a penurious parish nave,
a nave where endless obsequies are held,
because persistent rain prevents the coffin
from being brought out on the country roads.

The rain without me and within the hollow
clamour of a psalmist, louder and louder;
my conscience, by the water sprinkler aspersed,
is a cypress sorrowing in a convent garden.

Now my rain is flood, and I shall not see
the sunshine on my ark, because my heart
on the fortieth night must break for good;
my eyes preserve not even a faint gleam
of the solar fire that burned my corn;

my life is nothing but continuance
of exequies under baleful cataracts.

4

My Heart Atones . . .

My heart, loyal, atones in the darkness.
I shall bring it forth, like a tongue of fire
forth from a tiny purgatory into light;
and, hearing it thud against its prison, I drown
deep in the father's conscience-stricken love
who feels his blind son trembling in his arms.

My heart, loyal, atones in the darkness.
Joy, love, grief . . . all is laceration,
spurring its cruel logarithmic course,
its avid tides and its eternal swell.

My heart, loyal, atones in the darkness.
Mitre and valvule . . . I shall tear it out
to bear it in triumph to the knowledge of light,
the stole of violets on the shoulders of dawn,
the mulberry girdle of the eventides,
the stars and women's jovial entasis.

My heart, loyal, atones in the darkness.
Mine from a sheer pinnacle to cast it
a bleeding discus to the solar pyre.
So I shall extirpate my cancer of
exceeding weariness, suffer east and west
unmoved, and with perverted smile assist
at the ineptitudes of inept culture,
and flame will be within my heart inflamed
by the celestial sphere's symphonic fire.

5

Your Teeth

Your teeth are the fair excessive coast
along which smiles by compass navigate
as the tossings of sober gaiety list.

You smile gradually, as in the mantling
current of the tide sea-water smiles,
and totally, like an attempted *Fiat
Lux* for the night of mortals that behold you.
Your teeth are thus a jewel of great price.

Care them with care, for in such care inheres
no less transcendence than when a Pontiff touches
up his encyclic and burnishes his crook.

Care your teeth, conclave of hailstones, train
of foam, exhaustless ore, areopagus
of perfect astronomical minutiae,
manna sating retina and hunger
of the Twelve Tribes that hang upon your lips.

Your teeth in a rebellion would obtain
to serve the despot as zodiacal missiles
and turn discordant howls into a choral,
riot and fury into harmless frolics,
the insurgents into a concourse of the blind.

Under the secret arcades of your gums,
as in an infinitesimal aqueduct,
the worthiest mortal might with dignity
appease his parched desires . . . until the thunder
at the Last Judgement of the angel's trump.

Since all fair amulets are by the earth
engulfed, and since your idol's teeth must yet
glisten in the grim skeleton's grisly grin,
I enshrine them here, their clean design
and their divine nobility, for the amaze
and glory of gyratory mankind.

6

Wet Earth

Wet earth of liquid evenings when the rain
whispers and girls soften
under the redoubled pelting of the drops
on the roof terrace.

Wet earth of odoriferous evenings when
misanthropy toils up to the lascivious
solitudes of air and on them lights
with the last dove of Noah;
while the thunder crackles tirelessly
along the miry clouds.

Wet evenings of steaming earth when I
acknowledge I am made
of clay, for in its summer tears, beneath
the auspice of the light that is half gone,
the soul turns to water on the nails
of its cross.

Evenings when the telephone invites
naiads known for their knowingness,
who leave their bath for love,
to strew their fatuous tresses on the bed

and to lisp, with perfidy and profit,
damp and panting monosyllables
as the fine rain harries the window-panes. . . .

Evenings like an alcove under the sea,
its bed its bath;
evenings when a maiden
grows old in front of her extinguished hearth,
waiting for a swain to bring her a live coal;
evenings when on earth
angels descend to plough unerring furrows
on edifying fallows;
evenings of supplication and Pascal candle;
evenings when the squall
incites me to inflame
each frigid maiden with the opportune coal;

evenings when, my soul
oxidized, I feel
an acolyte of camphor,
slightly swordfish, slightly
Saint Isidore Labrador. . . .

7

The Malefic Return

Better not to go back to the village,
to the ruined Eden lying silent
in the devastation of the shrapnel.

Even to the mutilated ash-trees,
dignitaries of the swelling dome,
the lamentations must be borne of
the tower riddled in the slinging winds.

And on the chalk of all
the ghostly hamlet's walls
the fusillade engraved
black and baneful maps,
whereon the prodigal son might trace,
returning to his threshold,
in a malefic nightfall,
by a wick's petrol light,
his hopes destroyed.

When the clumsy mildewed key
turns the creaking lock,
in the ancient
cloistered porch
the two chaste gyps
medallions will unseal narcotic lids,
look at each other and say: "Who is that?"

And I shall enter on intruding feet,
reach the fatidic court
where a well-curb broods
with a skin pail dripping
its categoric drop
like a sad refrain.

If the tonic, gay, inexorable sun
makes the catechumen fountains boil
in which my chronic dream was wont to bathe;
if the ants toil;
if on the roof the crawy call resounds
and grows aweary of the turtle-doves
and in the cobwebs murmurs on and on;
my thirst to love will then be like a ring
imbedded in the slabstone of a tomb.

The new swallows, renewing
with their new potter beaks

the early nests;
beneath the signal opal
of monachal eventides
the cry of calves newly calved
for the forbidden exuberant udder
of the cud-chewing Pharaonic cow
who awes her young;
belfry of new-aspiring peal;
renovated altars;
loving love
of well-paired pairs;
betrothals of young
humble girls, like humble kales;
some young lady
singing on some piano
some old song;
the policeman's whistle . . .
. . . and a profound reactionary sorrow.

8

Ants

To warm life passing singing with the grace
of a woman without wile or veil,
to unconquered beauty, enamouring, saving,
responds, amid the magic hour's elation,
a rancour of ants in my voracious veins.

The pit of silence and the swarm of sound,
the flour cloven like a double trophy
on fertile busts, the Hell of my belief,
the rattle of death and prelude to the nest,
chastise the ceaseless truant formication.

But soon my ants will deny me their embrace
and from my poor and diligent fingers fly
as a cold bagasse is forgotten on the sand;
and your mouth, cypher of erotic prowess,
your mouth that is my rubric, food, adornment,
your mouth that in its flaunting tongue vibrates
like a reprobate flame escaping from a kiln
into a throng of bitter howling gales
where the moon prowls intent to ravish you,
your mouth will smell of shroud and crushed grass,
of opiate and respond, wick and wax.

Before my ants abandon me, Amada,
let them journey the journey of your mouth
to gorge viatica of the sanguinary fruit
provoking me from Saracen oases.

Before your lips die for my sorrow give
them to me on the graveyard's critical threshold,
their bread and perfume, venom and cautery.

9

The Tear

Over
the angular lily
that adorns the cadaverous pillow;
over
the hardened bachelor pain
of lying like a beardless congregationist
while the cats erect their clamour
and forge a bristling race;
over
the hunger never sated

of the lime that wears
light minds away
and the professional disenchantment
with which courtesans
spring out of bed;
over
marriage-making ingenuity
and the calamity that hopes for nothing;
over
the grave and the nest,
the bitter tear that I have drunk.

Tear of the infinite,
perpetuator of the amorous rite;
tear in whose seas
my anchor in its wrecked immersion joys
and I harvest the singular fleeces of
a rueful flock;
tear in whose glory the unfailing rainbow
of my punctual passion is refracted;
tear in which pennonless the masts
of consternation navigate;
tear with which my gratitude
sought to savour paradise;
tear of my shedding, I would be in thee
enclosed, and over me a tomb of joy,
like a look-out
in his briny morbid beacon-light.

10

I Honour You in Dread

Since your voice like a soft vapour laps me
and my eyes, offered to the eternal scythe,

dare for you to contemplate the coffin;
since to me your red sanctuary affords
a joy half chill, half cardinalate, before
the posthumous avalanche weeps upon the vane;
since the bold cervix of the ardent skeleton,
predestined to the brand of the funereal
walnut, has hurled for you defiance to Death;
I honour you in dread of a lost alcove,
necromantic, with your rigid face
ecstatic, on a shin, as on a pillow;
and since you are my blood's harmonious chosen,
Amada, and life's convulsions seem a bridge
above an abyss, on which we tread together,
my kisses scour you devoutly serried
over a sacrilegious cloak of skulls
as over an erotic domino.

11

Humbly

When the last weariness
comes upon me
I will to my village
like the stork in the proverb,
to kneel among
the roses in the square,
the hoops of the children
and the silken fringes of the shawls.

To kneel in the midst
of a grassy feast
where houseling

the clock in the steeple,
with its mourning face
and hands of gold,
and man and beast,
and the orange-blossom
that goes to the head,
and the rays of the sun,
on his chariot the All-Divine appears.

Meshed in the light
that evening spins
as in an apostle
spider's web,
I must say my fame
humbled and humble
more than the hooves
of the gentle mules
that are yoked to the Holy Sacrament.

"I know thee, Lord,
though thou goest incognito,
at thy scented tread
I am deaf and dumb,
palsied and blind,
that I may joy in thy balsamic presence.

"Thy sonorous car
of a sudden stills
the short-lived stir
as though the streets
were a playground wrapt
in a sudden hush.
My cousin, her needle
poised, behind
her window-panes
with statuesque gesture stands stock still.

"Bearer of
the news of the world
the village postman is plunged in his bag.

"Genevieve's damp bodice
hung out to dry
no longer dances
on the roof.

"The hen and her speckled
brood leave off
their fairy-tale.

"Don Blas his brow
is turned to stone
by the bulging slab
the ash roots crack.

"The oranges have
stopped growing and I,
to live this minute,
scarce quake before thee.

"Lord, my rash
heart that sought
proud chimerae
grovels and cries
that I am thy beholden chattel.

"Because thou hast set
in my breast a magnet
shaped like a clover
and the passionate colour of poppy.

"But that same magnet
is humble and hidden
like the magnetized comb

that maidens use
to catch up pins
and electrize their hair in the gloom.

"Lord, this chattel
with magnet heart
loves and confesses thee
with the root's
deep ardour thrusting
and splitting the age-old slabs.

"All is kneeling
and the brows in the dust;
my life is the passionate
poppy whose stem
effusive bends
to die beneath thy wheels."

Alfonso Reyes (1889–   )

1

The Menace of the Flower

Flower of drowsiness,
lull me but love me not.

How you profuse your perfume,
how overdo your rouge,
flower who kohl your lids
and exhale your soul in the sun!

Flower of drowsiness.

There is one resembles you
in your deceiving blush,
and too because she has
black eyelashes like you.

Flower of drowsiness.

There is one resembles you. . . .

(And I tremble alone to see
your hand in mine,
tremble lest you turn
into a woman one day!)

2

Tarahumara Herbs

The Tarahumara Indians have come down,
sign of a bad year
and a poor harvest in the mountains.

Naked and tanned,
hard in their daubed lustrous skins,
blackened with wind and sun, they enliven
the streets of Chihuahua,
slow and suspicious,
all the springs of fear coiled,
like meek panthers.

Naked and tanned,
wild denizens of the snow,
they—for they thee and thou—

always answer thus the inevitable question:
"And is thy face not cold?"

A bad year in the mountains
when the heavy thaw of the peaks
drains down to the villages the drove
of human beasts, their bundles on their backs.

The people, seeing them, experience
that so magnanimous antipathy
for beauty unlike that to which they are used.

Into Catholics
by the New Spain missionaries they were turned
—these lion-hearted lambs.
And, without bread or wine,
they celebrate the Christian ceremony
with their chicha beer and their pinole
which is a powder of universal flavour.

They drink spirits of maize and peyotl,
herb of portents,
symphony of positive esthetics
whereby into colours forms are changed;
and ample metaphysical ebriety
consoles them for their having to tread the earth,
which is, all said and done,
the common affliction of all humankind.
The finest Marathon runners in the world,
nourished on the bitter flesh of deer,
they will be first with the triumphant news
the day we leap the wall
of the five senses.

Sometimes they bring gold from their hidden mines
and all the livelong day they break the lumps,

squatting in the street,
exposed to the urbane envy of the whites.
Today they bring only herbs in their bundles,
herbs of healing they trade for a few nickels:
mint and cuscus and birthroot
that relieve unruly innards,
not to mention mouse-ear
for the evil known as "bile";
sumac and chuchupaste and hellebore
that restore the blood;
pinesap for contusions
and the herb that counters marsh fevers,
and viper's grass that is a cure for colds;
canna seeds strung in necklaces,
so efficacious in the case of spells;
and dragon's blood that tightens the gums
and binds fast the roots of loose teeth.

(Our Francisco Hernandez
—the Mexican Pliny of the Cinquecento—
acquired no fewer than one thousand two hundred
magic plants of the Indian pharmacopoeia.
Don Philip the Second,
though not a great botanist,
contrived to spend twenty thousand ducats
in order that this unique herbarium
might disappear beneath neglect and dust!
For we possess the Reverend Father Moxo's
assurance that this was not due to the fire
that in the seventeenth century occurred
in the Palace of the Escurial.)

With the silent patience of the ant
the Indians go gathering their herbs
in heaps upon the ground—
perfect in their natural natural science.

3

River of Oblivion

Rio de Janeiro, Río de Enero,
you were a river and are a sea;
what comes to you impetuous
forth from you languid goes.

Day ripens on your breast
in calms of eternity;
every hour you cull
turns to an hour and more.

Sponges of clarity,
your mountains filter the clouds,
and even the down you sift
that drifts from the wings of storm.

What trouble can resist you
when for every smart of salt
sweetness is in the air
and pity in the light?

The earth plays in the water
and with the city the field
and night enters
evening open wide.

The nightingale's song mingles
with the house's stir
and fruit and woman give
their single effluence.

To know you is to have
solitude of you

and in you to rest
of the rest forgetfulness.

The soul's disorder seeks
your limpid crystal law,
sleep showers from the nodding
crest of your royal palm.

For I am as the wanderers,
my home is in my pack,
I captain of a bark
with never a mariner's chart.

Río de Enero,
and I ask no better hap
in my mishap than to roam
your shores in the hour of wrack.

—The hand sustained the brow,
seeking to give it calm.
No, not the hand, the wind,
no, not the wind, your peace.

4

To-and-Fro of Saint Theresa

She weaves away at the bower,
sword shuttling in the loom,
branchy, hitherandthithering
Saint Theresa's moon.

The eyes in sparkling flight
caught among the lashes

free and captive give
battle and sue for peace.

A wizened darky trembles
entangled in his guitar,
a runaway bridegroom in
a slip of a wench's arms.

Wench in an hour won,
free though consenting, and alien.
How all flows, how all
departs whence all abides!

From the flowers' cups
drops of essence shed:
all in the instant that ends
in another is begun.

Below the sea escapes
in the same light it hales
and escaping never
escapes from the hands of earth.

On his lively mare the rider
of the air passes and passes
not: he bides in the shadow,
rowelling jingling spurs.

It is life journeyed through
as to a far remove!
A coming and going, a being
in flight and ever near!

A being beside me, and she
dead these years!
A deluding of all as by
Zeno with his arrow!

Time twines into the voice;
languor takes the song.
With agile feet the angels
suffer to come on earth.

Flying quiet moon,
heron self-ensnared,
in scrolls of leaves she moves
and moves not, wheels and wheels not.

5

Scarcely . . .

Sometimes an effluence rises,
made of nothing, from the ground.
Suddenly, hiddenly,
a cedar sighs its scent.

We who are a secret's
tenuous dissolution,
our soul no sooner yields
than dream wells over.

What a poor thing the wandering
reason, when in the still,
sunlight seems to fall
upon me from your memory!

6

Monterrey Sun

No doubt: the sun
dogged me when a child.

It followed at my heels
like a Pekinese;
>   dishevely and soft,
>   luminous and gold:
>   the sun that sleepy dogs
>   the footsteps of the child.

It frisked from court to court,
in my bedroom weltered.
I even think they sometimes
shooed it with a broom.
And next morning there
it was with me again,
>   dishevely and soft,
>   luminous and gold,
>   the sun that sleepy dogs
>   the footsteps of the child.

>   (I was dubbed a knight
>   by the fire of May:
>   I was the Child-Errant
>   and the sun my squire.)

Indigo all the sky,
all the house of gold.
How it poured into me,
the sun, through my eyes!
A sea inside my skull,
go where I may,
and though the clouds be drawn,
oh what weight of sun
upon me, oh what hurt
within me of that cistern
of sun that journeys with me!

No shadow in my childhood
but was red with sun.

Every window was sun,
windows every room.
The corridors bent bows
of sun through the house.
On the trees the coals
of the oranges burned redhot,
and in the burning light
the orchard turned to gold.
The royal peacocks were
kinsmen of the sun.
The heron at every step
it took went aflame.

And me the sun stripped bare
the fiercer to cleave to me,
    dishevely and soft,
    luminous and gold,
    the sun that sleepy dogs
    the footsteps of the child.

When I with my stick
and bundle went from home,
to my heart I said:
Now bear the sun awhile!
It is a hoard—unending,
unending—that I squander.
I bear within me so
much sun that so much sun
already wearies me.

No shadow in my childhood
but was red with sun.

Notes

Notes

FRANCISCO DE TERRAZAS (1525?–1600?)

The son of the Conquistador of the same name, Terrazas was considered "a most excellent poet in the Tuscan, Latin and Castilian tongues." In his few extant works—nine sonnets, one epistle, several *Replies to Eslava,* and fragments of the epic poem *Nuevo Mundo y Conquista* (The New World and the Conquest)—the influence of the great poets of his time, Herrera, Camões, and Ercilla, can be seen. Writing in the elegant and inventive style of Petrarch, he enjoyed a great reputation in his own day, as Cervantes' praise of him (in *La Galatea*) shows:

> Francisco, el uno, de Terrazas, tiene
> el nombre acá y allá tan conocido. . . .[1]

"acá," meaning in Spain, and "allá" in Mexico.

FERNÁN GONZÁLEZ DE ESLAVA (1534?–1601?)

González de Eslava was born in Spain, but his life and work both belong to Mexico—if it is possible, at such an early date, to draw a dividing line between Metropolitan Spain and the colonies. His plays, which represent the survival in America of the dramatic style current before the time of Lope de Vega, are remarkable for their skillful use of Creole and Mestizo turns of phrase. His religious songs carry on the tradition of the Spanish lyric (Montesino, Valdivieso). His lyrics and sonnets are good examples of skill and ease in the use of Renaissance forms. His plays and poetic works were published in 1610 (Spiritual and Sacramental Colloquies, Sacred Poems).

[1] The one and only Francisco de Terrazas, of great renown here and famous there. . . .

BERNARDO DE BALBUENA (1561 or 1562–1627)

Born in Valdepeñas, Balbuena spent his childhood and youth in
Mexico, returning to Spain in 1607. The following year he was elected
Abbot of Jamaica and in 1620 he was appointed Bishop of Puerto
Rico. He died in his diocese in 1627, having witnessed the siege and
sack of San Juan by the Dutch in 1625. He lost his house and his
library in the fire. His works were: *La Grandeza Mexicana* (Grandeur
of Mexico), 1604; *El Siglo de Oro en las Selvas de Erifile* (The Golden
Age in the Forest of Eriphyle), 1608, a pastoral romance in verse; and
Bernardo o Victoria de Roncesvalles (Bernard, or the Victory at
Roncesvalles), 1624, a great epic and imaginative poem.

La Grandeza Mexicana is a hymn to the capital of New Spain.
While almost all the Spanish poets of his time were disillusioned with
the world and wrote in praise of solitude—the solitude of the sage or
the lover, the shepherd or the knight errant—Balbuena glorified
society and common endeavor. His praise of the city is also the tale
of the passions which attended its building: ambition, the thirst for
glory or for gold, greed, and power. The prayers of the blind, the
preaching of the Friar, discoveries and conquests, the flourish of the
"cunning scribes' light quill," all these are the offspring of self-in-
terest, "the sun which gives life to the world." It is the creator of the
city and its culture, setting up the social hierarchy and giving rise to
the inevitable inequality of men. For Balbuena, the return to equality
is the return to barbarity. And in his poem he does not fail to men-
tion the source of the city's prosperity: the gold which

> entre el menudo aljófar que a su arena
> y a tu gusto entresaca el indio feo,
> y por tributo dél tus flotas llena.[2]

The critics have not given due consideration to this prophetic and
revealing social philosophy, nor to his attitude toward the Indian. On
the other hand, they point out that Balbuena is one of the important
figures of the Spanish baroque. The baroque of his style is original,
anticipating that of Góngora and Carrillo Sotomayor. His full and
sonorous lines, like a ship in full sail beneath the noonday sun, have
a splendor of their own. American by contact with the actual physical
world (as asserted by Quintana and Menéndez y Pelayo) or by the
laws of the cultural world (in the words of Henríquez Ureña), decora-

[2] Comes as the tiny pearls which the wild Indian digs from his sand at
your behest and brings as tribute to fill your fleet.

tive, enumerative, tireless, rich, varied, and monotonous in the very richness of his writing, Balbuena was the first to sing of the American world.

FERNANDO DE CÓRDOVA Y BOCANEGRA (1565–1589)

Born in Mexico, of Spanish descent, Córdova y Bocanegra became a Franciscan friar at the age of 21. Only two of his poems have survived: *Canción al Amor Divino* (Song of Divine Love) and *Canción al Santísimo Nombre de Jesús* (Song to the Most Holy Name of Jesus).

JUAN RUIZ DE ALARCÓN (1580 or 1581–1639)

Alarcón was born in Taxco, and began his studies at the University of Mexico, continuing them in Spain (1600–1606) and completing them in his native country (1609). In 1613 he left Mexico forever. In Spain he began his literary career as a dramatist. Lope de Vega's influence was then paramount in the Spanish theatre. The physical deformity of the hunchback Alarcón and his "Indian" origin (they always called him the "interloper"), certain features of his character (flattering courtesy, mocking obsequiousness, treacherous discretion, the malice of the maimed intellectual), and, above all, the novelty of his views on aesthetics, earned him derision, insults, and affronts. Alarcón enjoys the distinction of having been insulted and attacked by almost all the great Spaniards of his time: Góngora, Quevedo, Lope de Vega, Tirso de Molina, Vélez de Guevara, Suárez de Figueroa. They all planted their darts in the hump of his back. His passion for genealogy caused it to be said that "Don Juan's names proliferate like mushrooms. I can assure you that his humped back is full of them." Not content with their epigrams, the literary battalions took active measures: "The first performance of Don Juan Ruiz de Alarcón's *Anticristi* (The Anti-Christ) took place last Wednesday. They tried to upset the performance by hiding somewhere among the stalls, a little flask which gave off such a stench that many people who were unable to escape were overcome by the fumes." The authorities arrested Lope de Vega and Mira de Mescua.[3] Alarcón abandoned the theatre in 1626. He died in Madrid in 1639.

In comparison with the prolific works of Lope and Tirso, Alarcón's seems scanty: some thirty comedies. That is not the only feature which distinguishes him from his contemporaries. Alarcón was the creator of the comedy of manners and of character. Following the tradition

[3] Letter from Góngora to Master Hortensio, dated December 19, 1623.

of Terence, he had a direct influence on the French theatre in the persons of Corneille, Desmarets, and Montfleury. It is generally known that Corneille's *Le Menteur* is an adaptation of *The Suspicious Truth:* "et, s'il m'est permis de dire mon sentiment touchant une chose où j'ai si peu de part, je vous avouerai que l'invention de celle-ci me charme tellement que je ne trouve rien à mon gré qui lui soit comparable en ce genre, ni parmi les anciens, ni parmi les modernes" (Corneille).[4] Modern critics have written various studies of Alarcón's "Mexicanism." Those by Pedro Henríquez Ureña, Alfonso Reyes, and Antonio Castro Leal are outstanding.

MIGUEL DE GUEVARA (1585?–1646?)

The Augustin monk from the Province of Michoacán, Fray Miguel de Guevara, went among the Aztecs, Tarascos and Matlalzingos as a missionary, directed many priories, and was Provincial Visitor as early as 1604; his *Doctrinal Art and Method of Learning Matlalzinga for Administering the Holy Sacraments* (manuscript of 1638) included, among other poems, the famous sonnet, "No me mueve, mi Dios, para quererte. . . ."[5]

MATÍAS DE BOCANEGRA (1612–1668)

Bocanegra was a Jesuit born in the country. His *Canción a un Desengaño* (Song of Disillusionment) was very famous and much imitated in his own day. In spite of its length, many people still admire it. The first—and least conventional—part consists of a development of the theme of freedom, which resolves in the second part, along the theological lines characteristic of the period.

LUIS DE SANDOVAL Y ZAPATA (middle of the 17th century)

We owe the rediscovery of this admirable poet, who was very popular with his contemporaries but has been forgotten or treated with contempt until recently, to Alfonso Méndez Plancarte. Sandoval y Zapata left behind a prose work, *Panegírico de la Paciencia* (The Panegyric of Patience), 1645. No critical edition has yet been published of his

4 And if I may give my opinion on a matter which is really so little my concern, I must tell you that its invention delights me so much that there is nothing, in my view, comparable with it in its own style among either the ancients or the moderns.

5 I am not moved to love thee, my Lord God (Alfonso Méndez Plancarte, in his Introduction to the anthology *Poetas Novohispanos,* Vol. 1, Mexico, 1942).

poetical works, which are still scattered. His poems and those of Sor Juana Inés de la Cruz represent the finest flower of the baroque style in Mexico.

CARLOS DE SIGÜENZA Y GÓNGORA (1645–1700)

Sigüenza typifies the intellectual of the seventeenth century. Several of his traits mark him out as a forerunner of the eighteenth-century "intellect." His interest in the art and history of ancient Mexico, and his love for science (as revealed in his El Manifiesto Filosófico contra los Cometas [Philosophic Manifesto against Comets], and other writings) are proof of "modernity" as well as of the wide range of his knowledge. Sigüenza is an intellectual, witty, baroque poet. Góngora's influence merged with his own intellectual and historical interests. His long poem in honor of the Virgin of Guadalupe, Primavera Indiana (Indian Spring), 1668, is a good example of the rhetoric of the period.

JUANA DE ASBAJE (1651–1695)

Sor Juana Inés de la Cruz is one of the key figures in Latin American literature and one of the great Spanish poets of her century. She was born in San Miguel Nepantla, a small hamlet near Amecameca, at the foot of Popocatépetl. From childhood she displayed such a love of study that, to punish herself when she failed to learn anything, she cut her hair, since it would not be fair "for a head so empty of ideas to be covered with hair." At a very early age she appeared at the vice-regal court as lady-in-waiting to the Vicereine. Finding court life distasteful, and perhaps impelled by some disappointment in love, she decided, when scarcely eighteen years old, to become a nun. This is how she explains her decision: "I became a nun because, although I knew that I should find in that condition certain things—I am speaking of secondary matters, not of matters of substance—which would be distasteful to my mind, it would, in view of my absolute refusal of marriage, be the fittest and least unbecoming state that I could choose. . . ." In her cell, which was also her library, music room, and laboratory, she studied, received her friends, wrote or thought "so that while the pen was active, the compasses were still, and while the harp was plucked, the organ stood silent." She felt the thirst for knowledge but was also acquainted with love, though we can never know the story of the passion which breathes in her lyrics and sonnets. She did not find full freedom from the world in the convent: "She was beset with praise," as Alfonso Reyes says, "but also hostility, since in one way or another, they all wished to bring her down to their own level." Toward the end of her life, the Bishop of Puebla, concealing his identity under the pseudonym of Sor Filotea, sent her a letter bidding her lay aside her worldly learning and devote herself to religion. Sor Juana replied with her famous *Respuesta a Sor Filotea de la Cruz* (Reply to Sister Filotea de la Cruz), one of the most important documents in the history of Spanish culture and in that of the intellectual emancipation of women. Shortly after writing this admirable letter—the defense of her right to knowledge, the story of her vocation, and the derision of her fame—she sold her library, scientific apparatus, and musical instruments and signed two professions of faith with her own blood. Two years later, having renounced everything, she died nursing the sisters during a fever epidemic.

Sor Juana left behind various prose works, some of which have been lost. Apart from her *Reply*, her *Carta Atenagorica* (Athenagoric Letter), a piece of theological criticism, is remarkable. Among the lost works there is one whose title deserves mentioning: *El Equilibro Moral. Direcciones Praticas en la Segura Probabilidad de las Acciones Humanas* (Moral Equilibrium: Practical Directives for the Certain Prediction of Human Actions). How clearly the theme of moral doubt and that of freedom and obstruction are outlined in this title alone! Her plays consist of two comedies and three allegorical works on religious subjects, among which *El Divino Narciso* (The Divine Narcissus) is outstanding. The importance of her prose work—or rather, of the *Reply*—should not cause it to be forgotten that Sor Juana was above all a poet: an intellectual poet in *Primero Sueño* (First Dream); an easy, popular poet in her laments and songs; passionate and trenchant, or involved and witty, in her silvas, lyrics, and sonnets.

JOSÉ MANUEL MARTÍNEZ DE NAVARRETE (1768–1809)

Martínez de Navarrete was considered the most important of the neoclassical poets. He was a follower of Meléndez Valdés, and his poetical works are contained in the volume *Entretenimientos Poéticos* (Poetical Entertainments), 1823. Menéndez y Pelayo observes in his poetry "a certain melancholy fervor which marks the dawn of romantic sentiment."

JOSÉ JOAQUÍN PESADO (1801–1861)

A distinguished representative of the "academic" school, so called in opposition to the "romantics," Pesado was a correct and careful writer. Both his original works and his translations, particularly those of Horace and Tasso, are highly considered. A complete edition of Pesado's poems was published in 1886.

IGNACIO RODRÍGUEZ GALVÁN (1816–1842)

With Fernando Calderón, Galván was one of the founders of the Romantic school. Menéndez y Pelayo considered his *Profecía de Cuauhtémoc* (Prophecy of Cuauhtémoc) "the masterpiece of Mexican romanticism." In reality, this unsuccessful poet's talent came to light only in scattered lines and fragments amid the tangle of his verbose sentimentalism.

IGNACIO RAMÍREZ (1818–1879)

Ramírez is one of the outstanding personalities of the nineteenth century in Mexico. The life of the Necromancer, as he was nicknamed, was a constant struggle. As a student, he astounded his teachers and fellow-pupils by defending the thesis that "There is no God; natural beings are sufficient unto themselves." Journalist, teacher, soldier, political prisoner, Minister of Justice, member of parliament, leader of young poets, Latinist, he was one of the founders of Mexico. Late in life, old but unwearied and still vigorous, he fell in love with Rosario Peña and thus became the rival of a number of romantic poets, his followers and disciples. Ramírez' life was a contrast to his literary preferences. Though a radical in politics, he was a conservative in literature, and his poetry is frigid and correct. But the cold correctness of his verses is buoyed up from time to time by a stoicism not devoid of moral and human grandeur, even though it is very far removed from what is commonly described as poetic effusion. Ramírez' poems, comprising some fifty compositions, were published in 1889.

VICENTE RIVA PALACIO (1832–1896)

A Liberal journalist and lawyer, Palacio took up arms against Napoleon III's intervention and the Empire of Maximilian. He was a good soldier and became a general. When peace was restored he left the army and continued his literary career. A prolific writer, he was one of the popular novelists of the nineteenth century. The careless and picturesque prose of his novels and articles was abandoned for a purer style in a small volume of short stories, *Cuentos del General* (The General's Tales), which is perhaps the best of his works. His poems, which are few in number, are of good quality.

IGNACIO MANUEL ALTAMIRANO (1834–1893)

A pure-blooded Indian, and a peasant's son, Altamirano was unable to speak Spanish at the age of fourteen. He showed great promise at the primary school in his native village and won a scholarship to study in Toluca. There he made the acquaintance of Ramírez, who was a teacher at the school there. After a period of study and work, during which he earned his living by teaching French and managing a theatrical touring company, he came to Mexico City. In the capital he played his part in literary and political life beside Ramírez, his master, and the younger writers. At the outbreak of the Revolutionary war he took up arms, not to lay them down until the collapse of the Empire and the victory of the Republic in 1867. "With his accumulated army pay he founded the review *El Renacimiento* (The Renaissance) . . . and became the guide and teacher of two generations."[6] In 1889 he left his country to take up an appointment as Consul General, first in Madrid and later in Paris. He died in Italy in 1893. A follower of Ramírez and the master of Justo Sierra, Altamirano, the "Indian," was one of the group of intellectuals who not merely carried on the torch of culture at a time of great upheaval, but reformed that culture, fitting it for the modern world. He was a distinguished novelist and critic and produced a few poetical works; he represents the moment's pause when the balance between the romantic and the academic schools had been achieved. In both his poetry and his prose works he sought a kind of literary nationalism, kept in check by his classical education. The aesthetic tendencies of this writer can be seen in his descriptive poems of the tropical Mexican landscape. His poems were collected in a small volume, *Rimas* (Rhymes), published in 1880.

JOAQUÍN ARCADIO PAGAZA (1839–1918)

Pagaza, Bishop of Veracruz, a humanist, was one of the outstanding poets of the "academic school." In addition to his translations of Horace and Virgil, mention should be made of his well-constructed sonnets, in which he describes the landscape of the torrid zone of Mexico. His most important volumes of poetry are: *Murmurios de la Selva* (Forest Murmurs), 1887, *María*, 1890, and *Algunas Trovas Íntimas* (Some Intimate Verses), 1893.

6 Carlos González Peña, *History of Mexican Literature*, 1949.

MANUEL M. FLORES (1840–1885)

A member of the Liberal party, Flores fought actively as a young man until he was taken prisoner by the French invaders. Liberated by the Republic, he intervened in politics from time to time. He died blind and neglected in 1885. Flores' public life was only a very small part of his carefree existence, which was illuminated by a number of dramatic love affairs. Though he was the successful rival of Ramírez and Acuña, Rosario Peña was not the only, nor perhaps the most important, love of his life. Flores' eroticism sometimes brought him close to the very essence of poetry. In opposition to the academic tradition, still dominant, which attributed the value of a poem to the combination of vigor and discipline, Flores sensed that the essence of the poetic state is abandonment, dream, and love. Although he is the most gifted of the nineteenth-century Mexican poets, faults of taste and the lack of precision in his abandonment spoil much of his poetry. *Pasionarias* (Passion Flowers), a collected edition of his poems, was published in 1882.

JOSÉ PEÓN Y CONTRERAS (1843–1907)

Peón y Contreras was a romantic poet, carrying on the tradition of Duke de Rivas and Bécquer. His works are mainly dramatic and represent an interesting attempt to establish a national theatre. He is a polished poet. The most noted of his volumes of poetry was published under the title of *Echoes*.

JUSTO SIERRA (1848–1912)

Justo Sierra was a follower of Altamirano. He was Minister of Education for many years, founding the modern educational movement in Mexico and guiding the generation which was to bring about the Mexican Revolution (1910). Sierra's educational and cultural work was of decisive importance in the history of the country. The same may be said of his work as an historian and critic of Mexican life. In this sense he was the great descendant of the Liberals, and the forerunner of the present-day Mexican "intelligentsia." Deeply influenced by French civilization, he helped and protected the "modernist" poets, that is, the first Mexican writers to break with the influence of Spain and take an interest in the poetic experiments of the rest of the world, and particularly of France. Sierra's poems, showing the influence of the Spanish and French romantics, especially Hugo, are inferior to his prose and historical works. The National University of Mexico, which he founded, is now publishing his complete works, some of which provide essential material for any student interested in the history of ideas in Latin America.

MANUEL ACUÑA (1849–1873)

Of a gloomy and passionate temperament, Acuña committed suicide at the age of twenty-four. His career astonished his contemporaries and its conclusion filled them with consternation. Two of the most famous of Acuña's poems, supported respectively by the favor of the public and by that of the critics, are the *Nocturne* (dedicated to Rosario Peña) and his tercets *Ante un Cadaver* (Before a Corpse). Although Acuña's poems may seem to us empty and sentimental, we must surely see in him that strange fusion of love and death which is the hallmark of all poetry. Acuña is not a great poet, but his life typifies the poetic myth.

SALVADOR DÍAZ MIRÓN (1853–1928)

Gloomy and terrifying, Díaz Mirón is one of the "intractable" spirits of Mexican literature. Engaged in a constant struggle (with his passions, his fellow creatures, and his language), he was bound to fascinate and dismay his contemporaries, as the shadow of a bird of prey terrifies farm animals. He was as ruthless in his dealings with men and women as he was in cutting out a superfluous word or sacrificing an adjective. His accuracy with the pistol was not unlike the accuracy which gave his poetry its well-rounded metallic quality. But there were sometimes gleams of light in this dark soul. As he himself said, "a flash of lightning illuminates my gloomy spirit." Though he is not one of the great poets of the language, he is one of its most skillful craftsmen. Both romantic and classic, he influenced Rubén Darío and the first of the modernists, leaving posterity a book (*Lascas*, 1901) and a strict awareness of poetry. His complete poems (1876–1928) were published in 1941 (biography, notes, and bibliography by Antonio Castro Leal).

MANUEL JOSÉ OTHÓN (1858–1906)

Like Díaz Mirón, Othón was a recluse, but his solitude was that of the wise and not the haughty man:

abandono el rumor de las ciudades:
de mis desiertas soledades vengo
y torno a mis oscuras soledades.[7]

Following the Latin and Spanish classics, he carried on into the "modernist" period a restrained form of poetry employed almost exclusively for the description of landscape. Late in life, an unexpected love affair, which disturbed the regular pattern of his habits, revealed to him a region of the human soul of which he had previously known nothing. Thanks to that love, he discovered in fuller measure the natural scene of which he had sung before as an external observer, and found a strange but sure relationship between his mind and the northern scenery. In addition to his poems, which were his main interest throughout his life, Othón also wrote some plays and narrative prose works. His complete works were published in 1945.

MANUEL GUTIÉRREZ NÁJERA (1859–1895)

Gutiérrez Nájera was one of the pioneers of "modernism" in America. He founded the *Revista Azul* (Blue Review), and his poems and criticism reflect the general trends of that original group, in direct touch with the last of the French romantics and classics. Gutiérrez Nájera was one of the first "pure literati" of Mexico, thus breaking with the tradition of the Liberal generation. This poet had a great influence in his own day, and on the generation immediately following. With grace and melancholy he shakes the old timbers of the language. Many of his innovations went out of date extraordinarily quickly; what was then a smile now sometimes seems to us a grimace; but, had it not been for Gutiérrez Nájera, Mexican literature would have continued for many years to tread the mill of Spanish romanticism. He was an elegiac poet, an original storyteller, and a wise critic. Various collected volumes of his works have been published: his poetry, with a foreword by his friend and protector, Justo Sierra, in 1896; and his prose in 1898 and 1903.

FRANCISCO A. DE ICAZA (1863–1925)

Representing an original movement in the "modernist" school, he was influenced by the popular poetry of Spain and the German romantics. He was a distinguished critic, and much of his work deals

7 Forsaking the clamor of cities, I come from the lonely desert and return to my dim solitude.

with the Spanish classics: Cervantes, Lope de Vega, Gutierre de Cetina, etc. He translated Hebbel and Nietzsche. His poetic works are: *Efímeras* (Ephemerals), 1892; *Lejanías* (Distances), 1899; *La Canción del Camino* (Song of the Road), 1906; *Cancionero de la Vida Honda* (Songs of the Profound Life) and *La Emoción Fugitiva* (The Fleeting Emotion), 1925.

LUIS G. URBINA (1868–1934)

Urbina was a poet, critic, and essayist. Carrying on the "manner" of Gutiérrez Nájera in his first period, he later moved on to a purer and more sober style, becoming one of the best poets of the "modernist" movement in Mexico. He was an excellent critic, and Mexican literature is indebted to him for a number of memorable studies. He was also an excellent essayist and storyteller. His most important volumes of poetry are: *Puestas de Sol* (Sunsets), 1910; *Lámparas en Agonía* (Dying Lamps), 1914; *El Corazón Juglar* (The Juggler Heart), 1920, and *El Cancionero de la Noche Serena* (Songs of the Calm Night), 1941.

FRANCISCO GONZÁLEZ LEÓN (1868?–1945)

A poet of retiring disposition, González León introduced, in the very heart of the modernist movement, a colloquially intimate form of poetry not very unlike that at which Ramón López Velarde had aimed with greater brilliance. Conscious of the similarities between them, López Velarde gave his views on González León's poetry as follows: "His originality is the true originality of the poet—that of the senses." His poetic works are: *Campanas de la Tarde* (Evening Bells), 1922; and *De Mi Libro de Horas* (From my Book of Hours), 1937.

AMADO NERVO (1870–1919)

Nervo is one of the most influential figures in Latin American modernism. He was one of the founders of the *Revista Moderna* (Modern Review), which succeeded Gutiérrez Nájera's *Blue Review*. The *Modern Review* was the journal of the second "modernist" generation, which was particularly influenced by the French and Belgian symbolists. In his first period—*Perlas Negras* (Black Pearls), 1898; *El Exodo y las Flores del Camino* (The Exodus and the Flowers on the Way), 1902; *Los Jardines Interiores* (Internal Gardens), 1905—Amado Nervo proved himself one of the best poets of his school. At a later date—*En Voz Baja* (In an Undertone), 1909; *Serenidad* (Serenity), 1914; *Elevación* (Elevation), 1917; *Plenitud* (Fullness), 1918—his poetry became more intimate and less remarkable. He was a prolific writer and published various short novels, stories, and critical essays.

JOSÉ JUAN TABLADA (1871–1945)

A poet, art critic, and journalist, Tablada was one of the most fertile and questioning minds of his generation. A forerunner of modern poetry, he introduced the *haiku* into the Spanish language. His works and his example are still influential in Mexican literature. His first volumes of poetry are close to the "modernist" school: *El Florilegio* (Florilegium), *Al Sol y Bajo la Luna* (In Sunlight and in Moonlight). His later works belong to the contemporary Mexican school of poetry: *Un Día* (A Day—sketches); *Li-Po* (ideographical verses); *El Jarro de Flores* (The Vase of Flowers—separate lyrics), and *La Feria* (The Fair). As an art critic he was one of the first people to realize the value of Mexico's pre-Columbian past and one of the champions of modern painting (whether Mexican or foreign). Much of Tablada's work is still to be found scattered through periodicals and reviews.

ENRIQUE GONZÁLEZ MARTÍNEZ (1871–1952)

A poet who came between the end of "modernism" and the beginning of the contemporary school of poetry, González Martínez is another of the recluses of Mexican literature. His works influenced a few Mexican poets who personified the reaction against the poetry of the late nineteenth century. The significance of González Martínez' work for modern Spanish poetry has already been discussed in the introduction to this Anthology. The following works from his continuous stream of publications should be mentioned: *Los Senderos Ocultos* (Hidden Paths), 1909; *La Muerte del Cisne* (The Death of the Swan), 1905; *Parábolas y Otros Poemas* (Parables and Other Poems), 1918; *La Palabra del Viento* (The Words of the Wind), 1921; *El Romero Alucinado* (The Hallucinated Pilgrim), *Las Señales Furtivas* (Furtive Signs), 1925; *Poemas Truncos* (Truncated Poems), 1935; *Bajo el Signo Mortal* (Under the Sign of Death), 1942; *Segundo Despertar* (Second Awakening), 1945; *Babel* (1949). His complete works up to 1940 have been published in three volumes under the title of *Poesías.*

RAFAEL LÓPEZ (1875?–1943)

Represents the sensuous, sculptural movement in Mexican "modernism." He published only one volume of poetry—*Con los Ojos Abier-*

tos (With Open Eyes)—during his lifetime. Shortly after his death, another volume entitled *Poemas* was published, adding to his previous work without marking any radical change in it.

EFRÉN REBOLLEDO (1877–1929)

The author of *Joyeles* (Jewels), 1907, *Rimas Japonesas* (Japanese Rhymes) and *El Libro del Loco Amor* (The Book of Mad Love), 1916. The formal perfection of his poems is combined with an anguished eroticism. Apart from his volumes of poetry, he published various novels in which we can detect his tastes and the influence of the symbolists and classical writers.

MANUEL DE LA PARRA (1878–1930)

The poems of this melancholy poet have been collected in a single volume, *Visiones Lejanas* (Distant Visions), 1914, a continuation and refinement of the less sensual trends of modernism.

RAMÓN LÓPEZ VELARDE (1888–1921)

López Velarde is the most admired and most carefully studied poet in Mexico. His works are considered to mark the beginning of contemporary Mexican poetry. In the Introduction to this book an attempt has been made to analyze his significance. The volumes of his poems are entitled: *La Sangre Devota* (Consecrated Blood); *Zozobra* (Disquiet); and posthumously, *El Son del Corazón* (The Sound of the Heart). Some of his prose works have been collected in *El Minutero* (The Little Needle), invaluable as an aid to a better understanding of his mind. *El León y la Virgen* (The Lion and the Virgin, with a foreword by Xavier Villaurrutia) is a good anthology of López Velarde's works.

ALFONSO REYES (1889——)

Alfonso Reyes is regarded as one of the great contemporary writers in Spanish. It would be impossible to give a list of his prose works, which include more than a hundred volumes. His most important poetic works are: *Huellas* (Prints), 1922; *Pausa* (Pause), 1926; *Romance del Río de Enero* (Romance of Rio de Janeiro), 1933; *Yerbas del Tarahumara* (Tarahumara Herbs), 1934; *Golfo de México* (The Gulf of Mexico), 1935; *Otra Vez* (Once Again), 1936; *Cantata en la tumba de Federico García Lorca* (The Tomb of Federico García Lorca), 1937; *Romances*, 1945, and the dramatic poem *Ifigenia Cruel*

(Cruel Iphigenia), 1924. "Une étude méthodique de la littérature mexicaine d'aujourd'hui devra commencer par l'œuvre d'Alfonso Reyes. Œuvre de poète surtout, mais aussi de critique et d'érudit. . . . Polyglotte et voyageur, critique militant et portraitiste littéraire."[8] As a poet, he is the author of the *Visión de Anahuac* (Vision of the Anahuac)—"description minutieuse, comme un tableau de Breughel, de l'antique cité de Mexico, telle qu'elle apparut aux yeux des conquistadores. Description lyrique aussi, et d'un lyrisme qui rejoint par instants celui de Saint-John Perse. . . ."[9]

[8] Any systematic study of contemporary Mexican literature must begin with the work of Alfonso Reyes. It is above all the work of a poet, but also of a critic and a scholar . . . a polyglot traveler, a militant critic, and a literary portrait painter.

[9] "A description of the ancient city of Mexico as it was seen by the Conquistadores, reminiscent, in its minute exactitude, of a painting by Breughel. But a lyrical description, too, akin at times to the lyricism of Saint-John Perse. . . ." Valéry Larbaud, in his introduction to the *Visión de Anahuac* (N.R.F., Paris, 1927).

The Library of Congress has cataloged this book as follows:

Paz, Octavio, 1914—   *comp.*
    Anthology of Mexican poetry. Translated by Samuel
Beckett. Pref. by C. M. Bowra. Bloomington, Indiana
University Press ı1958ı

    211 p. 22 cm. (UNESCO collection of representative works:
Latin American series)

    1. Mexican poetry—Translations into English. 2. English poetry
—Translations from Spanish.   ı. Title.   (Series)

PQ7299.E3B4   861.082   54–7973

    Library of Congress